Dedication

To my wonderful daughter, Morgan. Thank you for giving my life such profound meaning. I love you so much more than words could ever begin to touch.

—Shannon O'Dowd

*The Ultimate On-Camera Guidebook: Hosts*Experts*Influencers*

Published by TVGuestpert Publishing

ISBN-13: 9780988585553
BISAC CODES:
PER010000
BUS052000

Nationwide Distribution through Ingram & New Leaf Distributing Company.

TVGuestpert & TVGuestpert Publishing are visionary media companies that seek to educate, enlighten, and entertain the masses with the highest level of integrity. Our full service production company, publishing house, management, and media development firm promise to engage you creatively and honor you and ourselves, as well as the community, in order to bring about fulfillment and abundance both personally and professionally.

Front Book Cover Design by Jonathan Fong
Book Design by Carole Allen Design Studio
Jacquie Jordan Headshots by Starla Fortunato
Shannon O'Dowd Cover Headshot by Shawn Smith
Shannon O'Dowd Back Cover/Insert Headshots by Courtney Lindberg
Host Headshots on page 17 by Courtney Lindberg
Expert Headshots on page 88 by Starla Fortunato and Suki Zoe

Edited by TVGuestpert Publishing

Published by TVGuestpert Publishing

TVG

11664 National Blvd, #345
Los Angeles, CA. 90064
310-584-1504
www.TVGuestpertPublishing.com
www.TVGuestpert.com
First Printing July 2019
10 9 8 7 6 5 4 3 2 1

THE ULTIMATE
ON-CAMERA
GUIDEBOOK
HOSTS • EXPERTS • INFLUENCERS
JACQUIE JORDAN AND
SHANNON O'DOWD

ACKNOWLEDGMENTS

I'd like to thank Carolyne Barry for being my mentor for over a decade … you are with me always and I can still hear your voice in my head telling me I can do it. I miss you so much. I'd also like to thank Blair Taylor for always seeing my shine and value even when I couldn't and being truly the best talent agent AND FRIEND a person could ever even dream to have. Suzanne Sena, thank you for all your guidance and support and really giving me the confidence that I could have a career in this field. And Tim Kessler, the first agent I ever met in this business. Your vision, wisdom and perspective is always so incredible and I'm proud to call you a friend.

I'd also like to thank Courtney Lindberg, Rosie Tisch, Kyle Kittleson, Mike Ganino, Tyler Banken, Kelley Bruggere, Alara Ceri and Jason Carter for not only years of being amazing work colleagues, but also for the years friendship (as well as being willing to contribute to this book).

Thank you to my soul sisters Nikki Carson and Lesley Demetriades as well as Brian McArdle for being a constant source of love and support. And to my parents, who fed the flame inside me and always made me believe anything was possible.

—Shannon O'Dowd

To Team TVGuestpert, the Guestperts, our Producers, the team that keeps our infrastructure strong led by Stephanie Cobian, Jonathan Fong, Rachel Quaill and Khala Quaill, Victoria Reynolds, Starla Fortunato, Randi Paige, Laura McConnell, Amy Porter, Jackie Petruzzelli, Suzette Cobian; all the workshop attendees of TVOnCameraTraining.com who have participated to help me develop my part of this content; the gang at New Leaf who put not just this book, but all of TVGuestpert Publishing's Books, in bookstores nationwide.

To all the contributors of this book, Amy Johnson, Adam Spiegelman, Phillip Andrew, Rebecca Bender, Susan Gold, Maria Singh, Tim Davis, Lisa Wolff, Carole Allen, and Lisa Haisha.

To Little Gracie Wiggles: I met you and Shannon on the same day. May your sweet little soul rest in peace.

To Shannon, thank you for sharing your talent and collaboration.

—Jacquie Jordan

PRAISE FOR
THE ULTIMATE ON-CAMERA GUIDEBOOK

The one stop shop for the modern day media influencer.

—*Mimi Brown, Producer, Good Day LA*

If you want to learn the art of on-camera work, learn from those who've mastered it. This is a must-read.

—*Chase Cain, 3-Time Emmy Award–Winning News Anchor*

This informative and essential tool for anyone who truly wants to be a success on camera is a must have. This book has a wealth of knowledge and an uncanny knack for pinpointing what makes a great on-camera personality. It is truly unrivaled.

—*Jason Carter, Host, Entertainment Tonight*

If you want to break into the world of hosting but don't know where to start, this book is a great resource to begin with. It's an essential learning tool for every host, no matter your level of experience.

—*Lea Zora Scruggs, Producer, BuzzFeed*

Read this book if you are an expert wanting to make the most of media opportunities or you're advising experts on media placements. A valuable tool chock full of years of experience and tried-and-proven formulas. And you won't fall asleep with density, it's a delightful read!

—*Susan Gold, Celebrity Talent Executive at Susan Gold Consulting*

This book is jam packed with all the information you need to successfully step into the world of on-camera hosting! A priceless resource!

—*Blair Taylor, Top LA Agent for Celebrity Endorsements/Product Hosts*

FOREWORD

It was 2009 and I just moved to Los Angeles from Detroit. My eager and inexperienced twenty-three-year-old self was going door-to-door to production companies to drop off my resume. As a Midwest kid with a dream of working in entertainment and no idea where to begin, drop-off resume number thirty-something-ish is when I stumbled up to a business directory in a Corporate Park. I found a business called TVGuestpert.

I had no idea what a TVGuestpert was, but I saw the letters "T" and "V", so I figured it was worth me popping in and saying "hello." I had no idea what Jacquie Jordan did. I had no idea who Jacquie Jordan was. I had no idea what to say to her. I had no idea how I could help. All I knew was that I was willing to learn.

That random, chance encounter lead to years of continual and successful collaboration. Not only have I been blessed with Jacquie's guidance and friendship, here I am writing a foreword in her book, *The Ultimate On-Camera Guidebook: Hosts*Experts* Influencers*, and this is a first look at how Hollywood works.

I can tell you that both these women, Jacquie and Shannon, are forces to be reckoned with both individually and together. As a two-time Emmy-nominated television producer, speaker, and media coach with credits that include Fox, ABC, CBS, YouTube Red, Facebook Watch, Netflix and many others, I have either produced the host, the expert, or the influencer at any given show, or I myself have been the host, the expert, or the influencer. That is why this information is so invaluable to you, the reader.

Jacquie doesn't just care about selling books. She doesn't just care about putting people on television. Jacquie cares about helping people discover who they truly are and then teaching them how to tell their message in a way that the world will understand, receive and be inspired. She's one of the most caring and passionate women I've ever met in my life.

Through Jacquie I met Shannon, the co-author of this powerful primer. I experienced the same level of care and service to others that I had witnessed with Jacquie, which makes sense that these two came together for one experienced book. Shannon is deeply committed to the success of her clients and helping them every step of the way.

These two women are passionate about sharing their knowledge. They cared so much about laying out every element of the TV on-camera process in this book that it really is the Ultimate On-Camera Guidebook.

Together they set such an incredible foundation for someone who is beginning their process with on-camera work, as well as providing advanced information for the experienced host, expert, or influencer that even the most seasoned can still sharpen their game.

It makes my job easier as a producer and a development executive if you, as talent, can come to the table with the information integrated into the core of your being before you and I meet in front of the camera or behind the camera. So I am here to say:

It's time to buy the book.

It's time to get into the work.

It's time to learn.

These pages contain valuable information from two extremely experienced, educated, and highly skilled communicators and industry Insiders.

Like any information in life, it's not meant to only live on a page, it's meant to be practiced and applied. Dive into the process. Get into the work. Have some fun.

I wish you the best of luck in your journey in being able to sell yourself, sell your story, sell your passion, and serve your audience in the most powerful way possible.

Enjoy.

—Phillip Andrew Barbb

Emmy-Nominated Television Producer

TABLE OF CONTENTS

INTRODUCTION

Shannon and I come from two unique but not so different backgrounds. While we both have solid producing experience, Shannon's strength and talent are from her years in front of the camera, as a host, spokesperson, and successful working commercial actress. What makes her successful? She's made a darn good living doing all of the above!

I am a two-time Emmy-nominated television producer and *New York Times*–bestselling publisher who's created a thriving business by expanding the brands and business platforms of my clients through a wide range of media exposure.

We met at a coffee shop the morning after I rescued a dog, and bonded instantly over a shared love of animals and our passion for helping our clients realize their true potential. Not necessarily in that order. (Sorry, poochies!) Shannon and I felt strongly that we both had an abundant amount of on-camera training power and resources to really help and empower others to be great on camera. It wasn't long before we decided to pool our resources, and shared passion, in the service of supporting hosts, experts, and influencers in making the most out of every media opportunity that arises, while also teaching them how to create their own opportunities.

I call being on camera "real estate." Shannon calls being great on camera your "money zone." It's too valuable an experience to learn *as you go* with the opportunities that you get.

I liken it to wanting to be a Major League baseball player. Who walks up to home plate in the majors with a bat and steps into the batter's box without ever having faced any pitcher before? No one. That would be insane, right? Instead, you start playing as a kid. If you're dedicated, you join your Little League team, you practice long and hard, and study the game as hard as you practice it. You dedicate yourself to getting better, and through a combination of skill, luck, and perseverance, you just might make it to "the show." You'd better believe that even professional baseball players, especially the star players, continue to hone their craft. Each at-bat becomes a test of their dedication and an opportunity to shine. That's why you'll find the greatest hitters before and sometimes even after the games, taking more swings. Practice may not make "perfect" (an unrealistic aspiration that's caused more than its share of neuroses, if you ask me), but it will make you the best you can be.

Our hope is that *The Ultimate On-Camera Training Guidebook: Hosts*Experts*Influencers* will be your practice guide to perfecting your craft, so that every at-bat of yours in front of the camera will be another opportunity to hit a home run in your chosen field.

Jacquie Jordan

OVERVIEW

*The Ultimate On-Camera Training Guidebook: Hosts*Experts*Influencers* is an invitation to be brave and be public. It's an A-to-Z, literally, of what is required before, on, and after being on camera. Using fun anecdotal stories from our respective journeys in the business, we will break down the elements of on-camera performances including auditions, branding, content, director, editorial, focus, green room, headshots, host influencers, jargon, kit, languaging, memorization, highlighted, on-air, performance, questions, rehearsals, social media, talking points, under performing, vernacular, w, x, y, and z!

This guidebook takes the talent from preproduction and behind the scenes, to the business elements that create opportunity and success, to the new frontier of the digital age, to the influencers who are (re)shaping our business as we write these words. Our invitation is to create congruence in your content, execution, and visibility in a manner that gets you, your message, and your business results.

As the authors of this book and your on-camera training coaches, we want to inspire, educate, and motivate, while eradicating all that is standing in your way of creating purposeful on-camera performances. Often we see all that gets too easily in the way of making a good performance. Much of it is from lack of education about the process.

For example, many authors have shared with me that they appeared on a national television show or popular radio show but that they didn't sell any books. In my professional experience, this is a direct result of how the authors handled their content on air.

We've heard so many stories of amazing experts who accidentally prepared for a major on-camera opportunity by trying to "calm their nerves" and therefore were too low energy during their appearance. You can't be low energy on camera. That is a mistake that can cost you future bookings. You have to find ways to work with your nerves and have them serve your excitement.

On the other end of the energy spectrum are our well-trained on-camera professional fitness instructors who sold $40,000 worth of a home exercise DVD product from one appearance on Fox News Channel. When the segment ran again, they racked up another $40,000 in sales. This far exceeded their expectations. That type of ROI, the performance measure known as Return on Investment, makes the investment in this process important.

Then there was that time when one of our doctor clients was offered the position of chief medical correspondent on a news station in a major market, which (no surprise) came directly on the heels of a super-prepared and well-executed appearance on the afternoon news. More recently, an interior designer client landed her own home renovation show after doing a DIY segment on a local morning show. If you set yourself up for success, it can open many doors.

We have an expression that on-camera training is like baseball spring training (we're big fans of baseball analogies around here). If you want to play in the Major Leagues, you want to practice like a professional, crafting your pitch, messaging, and execution (literally your entire performance) before every game.

WHY MEDIA TRAINING?

Media training exists to prepare you for interviews by members of the media. The goal of working with a media training coach is to understand how to excel at this process, and to feel confident and prepared before the mic is in your face (or being clipped to your lapel).

If you are someone who could be interviewed by the media because of your expertise or occupation, you need to have media training. It is important for any company/corporate spokespeople, professional actors and actresses, musical artists, athletes, executives, entrepreneurs, experts, and other public figures, as you could be called on for an interview for an upcoming event, launch, or opening, or even in a crisis management capacity (in the event something happens within your sphere that you need to explain, defend, or spin).

Comprehensive media training should consist of teaching you 1) on-camera interview technique, 2) how to develop a clear and compelling brand message, 3) how to create succinct talking points for your brand and expertise, 4) key sound bites for your brand, as well as how to speak in sound bites when being interviewed on a variety of topics, 5) how to prepare for each appearance so your message is compelling, on topic, and engaging, and 6) how to set yourself up for success in your media appearances by learning proper etiquette, protocol, and procedure from arrival at the location, to being on-air, to saying your good-byes and thank-yous when all is completed.

We approach the process of being interviewed as a practice of being present in the moment. This allows you to read verbal and physical cues, know your own money zone for your energy and intonation, and be comfortable playing with all the above when the ON AIR sign is flashing. It is a physical, kinesthetic practice. Being a great conversationalist, an extrovert, or a good public speaker does not automatically make you a good interviewee.

People often try to reduce on-camera training to being all about hand gestures, where to look, and how to sit. But really, it's about executing content. If you know what you are going to say, your hands will know where to be during the interview. You can never anticipate how much notice you'll have before you are called to be on camera, which means you always want to make sure you're ready, and so is your content.

Media interviews are unlike any other conversation you will ever have. You must "get in the gym" and learn with your body and mind how to work this new muscle and build your muscle memory so when the time comes for your next media appearance, your body and mind will work together and know what to do.

Remember, media appearances are about brand positioning and setting the stage for you to be the go-to person in your field on a national platform. Each one is very important and should be treated as such. You need to be clear about your overall objective with your appearance and make sure that each on-camera opportunity is working toward your overall goal.

Media training will not only serve you, your reputation, your career objectives, and your brand … it will also make you appear credible and professional to media outlets. This will put you in a stronger position to secure appearances in the future, as members of the media vastly prefer to interview experts who are prepared, have proper on-camera technique, and have a clear brand message with succinct sound bites and talking points.

The point of the training is to provide you with an understanding of the media interview process, refine your messaging, and polish your delivery.

Rebecca Bender of the Rebecca Bender Initiative was interviewed on *Megyn Kelly Today* on NBC in the morning and shared her challenging experience. She was prepared as far as having talking points and, from her understanding with the *Megyn Kelly Today* show, she had an expectation of what should be asked, answered, and honored. She was told that she was on as the expert and that she would be given the top of the show and five minutes to deliver her speaking points.

Rebecca's point of appearing on the show was to help other viewers learn from her as a leading expert; educating law enforcement and helping survivors rehabilitate. From Rebecca relaying her experience, what happened instead was that after sharing her personal story, she was given less than two minutes to share the wealth of her expertise before she was ushered off the set. We hear this story from too many experts. It usually follows the same cadence.

Rebecca explained that the first question was an off-limits question that pried into her personal story. She did her best to answer directly but was given no opportunity to pivot to what she was there to talk about. The screen time for her personal story and her expertise didn't balance out.

For me, in my experience as a television producer, a media trainer, and a regular guest expert, I can troubleshoot what happened without even needing to know the details of the content. I am setting this story up here to reinforce the necessity of having media professionals, such as publicists, managers, and yes, media trainers on your team to act as your advocate and firewall. It's very challenging to hold all positions in a booking at this level of national exposure. When you walk into a restaurant, you don't expect the same person to be chef, host, and dishwasher. Similarly, after being booked on a show, it's difficult to be the guest expert, the publicist (who acts as the intermediary), and your own media coach. It's hard to hold the bird's-eye view when you are focused on delivering the details.

In this particular instance with Rebecca, she has a personal story that qualifies her to be the expert. In *The Ultimate On-Camera Guidebook: Hosts*Experts*Influencers*, we define this as her "anchor story." She has evolved past the personal story and has cultivated an identity locked firmly in her expert capacity.

Rebecca's experience is not unique. For many experts and advocates, what is missing, misunderstood, and misconstrued is that from a media perception no personal story or anchor story is off limits, especially if this information can be found online. Her classification, from a television producer's standpoint, is that of an expert by way of personal story, or anchor story.

We had another example of this with one of our expert doctors. He had his first taste of fame when he was the first bachelor to be asked to exit on the very popular show *The Bachelorette*. He then capitalized on the momentum of his fame (or as he would say, infamy!) to write his book based on the fitness tips from other bachelors on the show.

While working with us at TVGuestpert, we wanted to shift the focus away from his playboy persona, which was obviously of value to a reality show audience but might actually detract from the expertise he now wanted to project. Instead, we played up his experience as a world traveler with a wealth of medical wisdom to share.

In one of his first television appearances after signing with us, he was surprised when the morning show showed a photo of him from *The Bachelorette*. They chatted a moment about his experience of being on the reality show, to my doctor's surprise.

Even though we didn't pitch this information to the show, or include it in our presented speaking points to the producers, it is still in his bio. If you Google-search our client, as every producer will do, this information is readily available. His anchor story was of interest to the producer and the show.

In another instance, we booked our sex addiction expert on *The Dr. Oz Show*. He and his wife were picked up by a car to be homebase guests. Our expert is a recovering sex addict. He and his wife have overcome his addiction. As a result, he is an expert and a therapist in helping other men and couples move through the pain and betrayal of sexual addiction. When the *Dr. Oz* producer had our client on the show, the first question asked was about how his addiction affected the marriage; it was up to our client to tie in his personal story or anchor story to his professional expertise.

This is not an uncommon story structure for any show. Survivors who are experts will always be of interest in the media initially because of their personal story. For myself, I have grown professionally in terms of mentoring business owners and entrepreneurs in growing their business, but I am still identified by my television producing credits, some of which were compiled over fifteen years ago.

Often when an appearance doesn't go well, an expert will demonize the medium of television itself, desperate to place the blame on anyone or anything other than him or herself. But the truth is that it's usually the expert's own naivety about the dynamic he or she is participating in that is the true cause of the mishaps and unhappy results.

An expert licking her wounds after a tough outing will say to me, "But the show had an obligation to give me the time and ask the questions they promised in advance." True. It's also true that if we've put information about ourselves or our businesses out there on the internet, on social media, or in our bio, then that content (which is what it is) is still fair game.

As a hosting coach at Shannon O'Dowd Media Coaching, I've had hosts that were adept at one area of hosting be totally thrown by an opportunity in another area of hosting that required a slightly different skill set. For example, an entertainment host was thrown off when called in to audition to be a commercial spokesperson. She was a great entertainment host, but did not have the tools to sell a product. Another client who had hosted several infomercials felt discouraged when she lost an opportunity to be a full-time host for QVC. She received the feedback that she had done too much of a "hard sell" with her product pitch. There are different styles and techniques appropriate for the different types of hosting. Instead of being discouraged by not succeeding at an opportunity in one of these areas, you could/should see it as a learning experience to discover what technique or nuance is appropriate in each genre and build that skill set within yourself.

ACT 1: HOSTS

CHAPTER 1

THE CHANGING CLIMATE OF HOSTING

If we had a dollar for every time an aspiring host has called Shannon O'Dowd Media Coaching or TVGuestpert and announced, "I want to be the next Oprah!", I'd have as much money as, well, Oprah. Please don't misunderstand me. I'm not making fun of anyone here. I am all about having the biggest vision and backing into the action steps to align with the opportunity.

The truth is there is only one Oprah. She came up at a very specific time period in television that cannot be repeated. She rose from local news to a local talk show in Chicago while talk show giant Phil Donahue was the one and only. Oprah was unique; she was a woman on television, and she was black. This happened in the late '80s. She was the voice of "I am one of you." It was a host posturing that was uniquely relatable and a departure from the white-man-talking-at-you hosting style. I loved Phil Donahue, but television up until that point had been dominated by men. Oprah was a breath of fresh air. Right time. Right place. Right talent. Trifecta!

When I hear someone proclaim she wants to be the next Oprah, I take it to mean that she wants to be a great recognizable interviewer. That's fine, but I challenge her to put the amount of work into this desire that is actually required. Very few people are willing to do this.

You've already read in our Overview that our office says all great athletes practice in their off-season. If you want to be the great recognizable interviewer of your own energy signature and style, then put the time into what it takes to become that host. I subscribe to the "if you build it, they will come" approach to all hosting endeavors. Let's take a look now at what you need to do to "build it" properly.

BEST HOST

Like Shannon, who has the privilege of training so many great and talented hosts, I have had the privilege of producing some amazing hosts. One of my favorites was Jeff Probst. I was a producer on two of his shows at FX. This was before he hit his fame as the rugged, disarming, super-likable host of the Survivor series.

Even in his early days, Jeff was skilled at being on camera. You could give him a cue to cut his intro by four seconds and he could give the exact same take, in the exact same cadence, flawlessly, four seconds shorter. I've rarely seen news reporters that good with time cues. I would throw Jeff the line with one or two words deleted, and he could take it from there.

Two other amazing hosts with whom I've had the privilege of working are brother-and-sister duo Donny and Marie Osmond. It's one thing to be the solo host of the show, but it is an entirely different challenge to share airtime with a co-host without running the chance of stepping all over each other or creating too many pauses in the conversation waiting for the other person to speak. As their producer, I was able to capitalize on the great timing, humor, and banter they exhibited in their off-screen lives. I made sure they never grew too polished or professional to retain their charming and authentic sibling dynamic. I was honored to have my work with Donny and Marie recognized with two Emmy nominations.

One host with whom I worked on a daytime talk show was a great celebrity guest, but she turned out to have huge challenges when it came to hosting her own show. Specifically, she never seemed to grow comfortable with allowing the guest to drive the content. This host excelled at being a funny storyteller, but talking about herself in the host capacity was not what was required from that seat. Instead, she needed to prompt the guest to be a good storyteller. Things digressed so badly with this host that I started giving cue cards to the guests to help move the segments along. Finally, the studio paid her out of her hosting contract, just to get rid of her.

Moral of the story—being a good guest doesn't translate necessarily to being a good host. Or vice versa, as Shannon knows all too well!

It's important to acknowledge the swiftly changing climate of how viewers consume their content. I predict that the word "TV" is most likely going to be an antiquated one in the not-too-distant future, with digital streaming being THE way viewers consume content. With this evolution, the role of a TV host is also changing. And with social media, we are all able to have a platform and an audience now. Essentially, anyone with access to a smartphone (i.e., everyone you know) has the ability to be a TV host. Notice I said the "ability" and not the "talent."

There was a time when someone could just be a "host." You didn't need to be a celebrity or an expert in your field who is also good on camera. You could just be a really good host and you could have a career! A great example is Tom Bergeron of

Dancing with the Stars and *America's Funniest Home Videos*. With the exception of our beloved entertainment reporters (like Mario Lopez and Nancy O'Dell) and our game show hosts (like Pat Sajak and Alex Trebek), Tom Bergeron is one of our last great hosts on network TV who is only a host, not an expert or a celebrity, when he booked these shows. He delivered content in a fun, dynamic, believable way. That was what you needed ten to fifteen years ago to have a hosting career on TV. That's not to say that being a great host is easy—it's quite a skill! But if you were a great host, you had a chance to host your show on broadcast television. That rarely happens anymore. Even game show host jobs are now being given mainly to celebrities. Audiences want to see experts in their fields and high-profile people as the face and leader of unscripted content (as opposed to a scripted television show where the parts are played by actors).

I don't say this to discourage you, but to provide you with some modicum of realism when thinking about how to strategize for your own career. It's very important these days to not only be great on camera, but also to have a thing that can be branded as your area of expertise. For example, about ten years ago, I worked all the time as a host. I'm proud to say I became a really good, constantly working host. But my competence as a host doesn't mean as much in this changing climate. Now, I've also had to pivot and look to find areas where I could be seen as an expert. My agents have had to do this for me too. I'm now pitched as a "working mom" in the world of commercials, infomercials, industrials, shopping channels, etc. (which, believe it or not, is an expertise), as well as a media and pop culture expert in the news, morning show, and reality show realms. Since I have been a media trainer for over a decade, being a media expert was my most obvious fit. The industry needs to be able to know where you fit and how they can spin/pitch what you do. In these times of lightning-fast internet and instant gratification, you need to be able to quickly show who you are and what you can be counted on to deliver.

Now that digital platforms have given everyone the opportunity to create content, it's important to look at what areas appeal to you and where you want to make a contribution. Do you think you might be a good fit on YouTube? Is visual or shorter content more your style and you think Instagram might work well? Do you think you'd do well thinking on your feet and want to throw your hat in the ring for live streaming, on a platform like Facebook Live? Where are the other people in your area of expertise thriving? Who is your audience and where are they looking for content?

These are the kinds of questions you want to ask yourself as you start to map out your path to becoming a host.

CHAPTER 2

HOSTING STYLES

For all of you out there who consider yourselves aspiring TV hosts, no matter where you are on the hosting spectrum (maybe you've just gotten started, or maybe you've done a few jobs), it's important to remember that there are so many more areas of hosting than most people realize. If you're wondering how you could possibly make a living doing this if you're not Oprah Winfrey or Ryan Seacrest, the answer is to be patient, find your voice, and pick a path, any path, then stick with that path as if your career depended on it!

ENTERTAINMENT REPORTING: This includes red-carpet hosting and press junkets, along with shows like *Entertainment Tonight* and those on the E! network. Think of hosts like Mario Lopez, Maria Menounos, and Nancy O'Dell.

TALK SHOWS: You will also know these as national morning shows, daytime talk shows, and nighttime talk shows, though web talk shows and regional morning shows also fall into this category. National morning shows like *Good Morning America* and the *Today* show are good examples; however, there are regional morning shows in most major markets as well. Daytime talk shows include *Dr. Phil*, *Steve*, *The Ellen DeGeneres Show*, *The Wendy Williams Show*, etc. Nighttime talk shows like *The Daily Show*, *Jimmy Kimmel Live*, *The Late Show*, *The Tonight Show*, and *The Late Late Show* are great examples. Trevor Noah, Jimmy Kimmel, Jimmy Fallon, Stephen Colbert, and James Corden are great examples of late-night talk show hosts. As you can see, even though these are all under the umbrella of talk shows, there are hugely different styles and talents that are required and appropriate for hosts in each of these categories.

REALITY TV: Reality TV includes travel shows, fixer-uppers, game shows, competition shows, etc. When we think about reality TV hosts, we might think about competition shows with hosts ranging from Jeff Probst of *Survivor*, to Tom Bergeron from *Dancing with the Stars*, to Ryan Seacrest from *American Idol*. Hosts such as the late Anthony Bourdain (who was an icon in the travel show space), Guy Fieri of *Diners, Drive-Ins and Dives*, and Andrew Zimmern of *Bizarre Foods* fall into this category. For makeover shows, great examples are Jonathan and Drew Scott, aka the *Property Brothers*, and Joanna and Chip Gaines from *Fixer Upper*. Mike Rowe and Bear Grylls are great examples of TV hosting in the docu-reality space (shows that have a documentary delivery and feel). When it comes to game shows, icons like Pat Sajak and Alex Trebek are most people's first thought, though now we have celebrities like Jamie Foxx, Ellen DeGeneres, and Drew Carey occupying this space as well.

These are the typical areas that come to mind when most people think about hosting work. Now let's talk about some areas you may not have thought of or known even existed.

SHOPPING CHANNELS: There are also shopping channels like QVC and HSN. Usually those networks pay you six figures to start and it's a full-time job, it's reliable income, and it gives you a taste of what it's like to be on-camera talent (which is kind of what we all want, right?) Even though these hosts may not be household names for everyone, they are celebrities in their own right, and people who watch these channels are HUGE fans of the hosts and love to call in and follow their favorites. Also, people do get their start here. Mike Rowe was originally a QVC host.

INFOMERCIALS: Now you probably knew about infomercials, but you probably didn't know how great they can pay. They can reach up to $10K to $20K just for the shoot day and, on top, can often include quarterly payments or a percentage of profit. NOT BAD! Infomercials are also huge internationally. Turns out people in other countries love to hear Americans talk about products, because Americans really represent consumerism to the rest of the world. A handful of celebrities host infomercials for their products, including Cindy Crawford, Suzanne Somers, George Foreman, Christie Brinkley, Chuck Norris, and Richard Simmons. There are also some notable hosts who are celebrities in the infomercial world just for being very successful direct response hosts. Direct response is what the industry calls infomercials. Hosts like Forbes Riley, the late Billy Mays, and Vince Shlomi became big names in this space.

INDUSTRIALS: This is a wonderful area to start in if you are a new host looking to get some experience and footage for your reel. An industrial is an internal video for a company about their product or service, or a training video. The great thing is that it's internal, so it will never be broadcast on TV, and you can do a lot of them! It's usually just a video housed on the company's website. The pay is a decent: $1,000 to $1,500 for a day's work. Be careful to limit the usage to one or two years max with the right to renew. Even though it's internal, you don't want the company to have rights to use your image forever. Also, make sure to get a guarantee that they will send you the final video once it's completed so you can use portions of it for your reel.

TRADE SHOWS: There are also trade shows, which usually offer one to three days of work. Some of the best-known trade shows in the US are CES in Las Vegas and Comic-Con in San Diego. Trade shows typically pay a $1,000 to $1,500 a day and often have you traveling all over the country; sometimes you may travel all over the world live-presenting, and that really keeps you on your toes. I always say trade shows are kind of like the gym of hosting. Plus, shopping channels scout from this world a lot because if you are successful as a trade show presenter, that means you are adept at talking about products live, which is the exact skill set you need to be successful as a shopping channel host.

**Please see the ear-prompter section for some great tips for this area of hosting, as a lot of trade-show presenting work involves the use of an ear-prompter.*

PERFORMANCE DIFFERENCES FOR EACH AREA OF HOSTING

Entertainment Reporting

I have so many clients with news backgrounds come to me looking for gigs as an entertainment reporter. Their attitude is basically, "Hey, I did the hard news already, shouldn't the soft news be a piece of cake? I mean, really, Shannon, what's the difference?"

Well, I'm glad you asked, aspiring entertainment journalist! There is a difference, even if you don't realize it. When you're a newscaster, you're reporting on the news; when you're an entertainment reporter, you're reporting on entertainment. This may not seem like a big difference, but in terms of performance style, it's significant. When you're "reporting" on entertainment, you have to be a little bit more entertaining yourself!

For example, the first line is said like a title but also has a very "Extra, Extra! Read all about it!" to the delivery. Entertainment reporting requires an injection of personality not required for regular news reporting. We want to see how you feel about what you're talking about ... that's a key difference.

When you're reporting on pop culture, we need to be able to see how you tick and how excited you get about what you're reporting. If you put some more personality into that reporter cadence, you're probably going to be in the right zone.

Many aspiring entertainment reporters will have to work their way up the ranks doing red carpets.

Host Tip: When you're at these red-carpet events and given your handheld mic, always use the hand closer to your interviewee to hold the mic if you are in the shot. Crossing your body and going into profile to give your guest the mic is a no-no!

Reality TV

There are so many areas that are considered reality TV, including travel shows, makeover shows, competition shows, etc., it's hard to say there is one right way to deliver a script in this world. I will say that in general, the reads are way more natural and conversational for reality shows (with the exception of game shows). It's also important to remember that in reality shows you are often on-location somewhere, so taking in and giving us tastes of the visceral experience you are having is a crucial part. This is not the case if you are in a studio, but if you are in sub-Saharan Africa, we want to know what that's like. So taking in your environment (the sights and smells) is a great thing to do.

Another great thing to do when you are preparing for an opportunity on a reality TV show is to figure out what the writer and show producers intend for you to do and where to be. You need to get into the mind of the writer and deliver the copy the way he or she intended. This translates to asking what the tone of the show is, what type of host is needed, and how that host needs to relate to their audience in order to best serve the show. There are many versions and facets to your personality. Which side of you would be best for this project? What delivery style is needed? Start to prepare and rehearse from that space. This is obviously true for many types of hosting work, but I find it to be especially relevant in this area.

Talk Shows

This is a wonderful format if you have the gift of gab and love the art of conversation. However, most people don't realize what a skill it actually is to be a great talk show host. In addition to being great at banter, you must be incredibly skilled with transitions and hitting everything required of you in a block while making it all look like it's fun conversation. You might have seven minutes until a commercial break and have to cover a number of things given to you. But you must also freely chat with the audience after giving them that piece of information and find a way to casually move them on to the next topic effortlessly and seamlessly. It is an art. Seeing someone do it masterfully firsthand is truly awe-inspiring.

You will need to be a great interviewer to be successful in this space. This requires being genuinely interested in what your guests have to say, as well as being able to weave their answers into the follow-up questions you are supposed to ask. Making your guests feel like you hear them, enjoy them, and are having a conversation with them instead of just drilling them with questions is paramount to a good interview.

Being a great expert on television does not necessarily translate to being a good talk show host or interviewer. Holding the cadence, timing, and execution of a segment to a show in your head while you are listening to your prompts and cues from your guest is a well-practiced art form.

The one thing you need to consider if you are interested in entering the world of talk shows is that it will require you to be vulnerable, share yourself, and let your audience get to know you. This is a relationship between you and the viewers, and they tune in to catch up with their friend (you). If you are uncomfortable talking about how your child won't do his homework or how your bathroom always looks like a bomb just went off, this probably isn't the area for you.

Infomercials

The thing that I think really trips people up in infomercials (or direct response spots, as they are called in the industry) is the idea, "I've got to sell, I've got to sell, I've got to sell." That kind of puts you in a very cheesy, inauthentic space. As viewers, we feel put upon and we don't trust you. However, if you go into infomercial copy and you think during your performance, "I want to help you … I want to help your life to be better, easier, more affordable, or more fun and this product will do it," then you can approach the copy in that way. It really makes the delivery more genuine, and it puts you in a better performance space. Anytime you're presenting, or representing, any kind of product on camera, it really helps when you come from the space of how you can make someone's life better and how you can help. In other words, you're providing value, NOT selling!

When you perform product/service-driven copy (whether it be infomercial, industrial, or commercial spokesperson copy where you are delivering lines directly into the camera), you need to establish a connection with the person you are talking to about the product or service. Think of someone specific in your life with whom you would actually share this product or service in a regular conversation. This will help "personalize" your read.

Everything in infomercials is problem/solution. The host sets up the problem and then explains why the product is the solution. In the beginning of the copy, you establish that there's a problem in the way that you say it. For example, with the line "For those occasions when you don't want to deal with carrying a handbag or clutch, go with the Girly-Go-Garter," the way you say "those occasions that you don't want to carry a clutch" is the problem and "go with Girly-Go-Garter" becomes the solution. All that you're doing is creating the need in the viewer's mind.

Another thing you will find in scripts about products/services is that there tends to be lists. A wonderful trick that the great Suzanne Sena taught me was that when you are listing things, you either make sure to build the list with excitement and enthusiasm, or you make each thing on your list different by the way you say it. If not, you will more than likely lose your audience with a list that rambles on.

Lastly, it's important to figure out what stands out about the product or service you're promoting from other competitive brands in the same space in the marketplace. In other words, what makes your product:

1 Better
2 Different
3 Unique
4 More affordable
5 Easier
6 More fun

Those things need to be emphasized in the delivery of the script so we REMEMBER why this product is superior to its competition. I'd suggest not delivering your copy until you believe all of the above—authentic excitement is contagious, and will help you get hired a lot quicker!

Host Tip: *MANY performance tips from infomercials can also be used in the world of industrials. They are often very similar in approach. You may need to be more informational and buttoned up in an industrial spot, but there are a lot of similarities, as both are product/service-driven content.*

SHOPPING CHANNELS

Here is a loose overview of how shopping channels structure their programming, how you can deliver within the format in the role of the host, and some tricks of the trade that will put you a step ahead of the competition! Again, this isn't the exact order of how you need to present and you don't have to hit every single thing below, but it is a general format.

Shopping Channel Host v. Guest Expert

You will notice that most shopping channels usually also have a guest expert or brand ambassador there on behalf of the product being sold. It's their role to support the host and provide any information about the product the host may not know. This can be the owner/inventor of the product, someone hired from the company to represent it, or even someone who has gone through training to speak on behalf of the product and company. Their job is to be dynamic and help the host communicate the features and benefits of the product. Guest experts do NOT list item numbers or price, take phone calls, or open or close the segment. They are the guest of the host's show and are expected to stay in that role. This doesn't mean that they should not have speaking points prepared and an idea of what they want to communicate, when, and how. But it does mean that it's their role to be the guest in the host's home and allow the host to be the lead.

1 "Hello! Welcome back to QVC/HSN, your Shopping Headquarters. I'm Harriet Hosterson."

a "The next item we have for sale is Flashy Lashes, the last lashes you'll ever need to wear!"

b THEN problem -> solution -> product OR offer the problem, then introduce the product and solution (be sure to talk about what this means to the viewers and why they should care).

2 Item number and price! This is not usually included in the audition for these networks.

3 The hosts on these networks do talk about deals like "Interest free for $_ and if you put it on your QVC/HSN card, you get reduced shipping and handling!" OR "Today's Top Value," but you will usually skip this during the audition process. It is good for you to know, though.

4 Story -> feature . We don't just want a list of all the product specifications. Build a story or personal anecdotes around features to make them more interesting so we don't just tune out.

5 Tour the product. How does it feel, taste, smell, etc.? The best way to do this is to look at the product and think of all the questions you might have if you were buying it as a consumer. Put it in their hands!

6 Figure out what it does and all the problems it's addressing and then create stories to weave. For example, from the Flashy Lashes above: "You'll never have to worry about mascara running or flaking on you again!" (problem it solves) "I can't tell you all of the mascaras I've gone through that have flaked all over my undereyes or ran down my face when I sneezed. It can be such a mess!" (story to support the problem)

7 You are always talking to "HER," as your demographic is made up almost entirely of women, ages forty and up. Remember, this means speaking to one person! Avoid "you all," "everybody," "everyone," etc.

8 You want to take a casual, conversational tone and presenting approach. That means speaking at a warmer, slower conversational pace, as if you are talking to an acquaintance you want to get to know more and become friends. This is NOT a hard sell!

9 Don't overwhelm with facts and figures. Think about explaining things in a way that your grandmother would be able to follow.

10 Be self-deprecating and always assure your audience you're on their team. Examples: "I'm no tech wizard. If it has more than three steps, I'm done!" "We moms need to stick together." "Hey, if you're like me, you're a little klutzy."

11 Finish all your thoughts. Slow and clear. No shortcuts.

12 Some great phrases that really work are: "One of the things I love about fashion is___." "One call or click and you get everything you need (bundle)." "You will love this when you get it." "When you open this box you will be so excited." "There are times when TV doesn't do a product justice, and let me tell you, girlfriend, this is one of those times!"

13 With clothing, always include what you are doing when you're wearing it, how you feel, accessory options, and care instructions. Paint a picture for your audience, and make sure they can see themselves smack in the middle of it!

14 How does this product make people's lives more fun or more affordable, give them more time, or make their life easier? Hit on those things!

15 Focus on what makes this product unique/different/special among similar products. In the industry, this is called USP, or Unique Sales Proposition. What need does it serve, and how does it serve that need in a better way than all its competition?

The Top 50 Power Words that Sell

1. Absolutely
2. Accomplish
3. Achieve
4. Benefit
5. Best
6. Clear-cut
7. Compelling
8. Convenient
9. Critical
10. Dependable
11. Easy/Easily
12. Ensure
13. Exciting
14. Free
15. Fun
16. Guarantee/Guaranteed
17. Health/Healthy
18. How-To
19. Improve/Improved
20. Instant/Instantly
21. Love
22. Money
23. More
24. New
25. Now
26. Personalized
27. Power/Powerful
28. Private
29. Proven
30. Quality
31. Quick/Quickly
32. Results
33. Safe/Safely
34. Save
35. Secrets
36. Secure
37. Shocked/Shocking
38. Simple
39. Solution
40. Step-by-Step
41. Strong
42. Top
43. Uncover
44. Unique
45. Unleashed
46. Unlimited
47. Unlock
48. Winning/Win
49. Yes
50. You/Your

CO-HOSTING

Co-hosting is a huge part of hosting. To paraphrase the old kindergarten teacher's maxim, you have to be able to *play in the sandbox well with others* on screen. It's actually a little more challenging than it may sound. Below are some techniques to help you really shine as a co-host, both while being tested for the job and after you nail the audition and are sitting in the co-host's chair.

ACKNOWLEDGE YOUR CO-HOST: If you have the first line, it is your duty to acknowledge your co-host within the first five seconds of starting the spot. Even if it's not written into the script, you need to look over and make clear to the viewer that you and your co-host are a happy, well-oiled team. Think of this as a three-person conversation between you, your co-host, and the viewer. It is rude not to introduce us to the other person in the conversation right away. You wouldn't do it if you were co-hosting a party, right? So don't do it when you're co-hosting a show!

PROXIMITY: When you are co-hosting and standing up, you should be close enough that you are almost, but not quite, touching your co-host or guest. This may feel weird at first. After all, having a few feet in between you and the person you're talking to is normal in real life, but those few feet look like miles on camera. Also, try to keep your body positioned flat to the camera, not too angled to each other. If you are seated, make sure to be pretty close as well, with a slight (about 10-to-15-degree) angle toward each other.

USING YOUR HANDS: If you are auditioning, you might be holding a script, and if you're on location shooting, you might be holding a mic. Regardless, try to hold your prop, script, notes, or mic with the hand that is closer to your co-host so you have your other hand free to emote and gesture without having to worry about hitting your co-host.

STAY OUT OF PROFILE: In life, we turn and face the person we are talking to, right? Well, this is not the case in co-hosting. If you did this, you'd spend your whole performance showing the camera and viewer only half of your face (your profile). In co-hosting, you need to stay flat to the camera and just do a slight face tilt and look at your co-host mostly with your eyes. It can feel unnatural at first, but it's technically the best way to handle co-hosting. I'm not suggesting you try this technique in life, unless you're trying to freak out your friends. But the camera, and your producers, will love it!

CREATING RELATIONSHIP: One of the main goals of co-hosting is to make it look like you and your co-host have been working together for years. If the two of you are just meeting at a screen test or audition, ask five or ten personal questions about your co-host's life, upbringing, family, hobbies, etc. to accelerate the process of getting to know the person better. Someone with any experience at all should do the same with you. Even if none of this comes up in what you say on camera, it will register in the body language that you are not strangers.

UTTERS & MUTTERS: A fantastic way to create the sense of a conversation happening is doing an utter or mutter before your line as a reaction to what the other host just said. It's a great way to practice the "Yes, And!" skills they teach in improv. Essentially, you're letting your co-host know you heard what he or she said, acknowledge it (the YES), and are adding to it (the AND). For example, if your co-host just said, "Nicole Kidman was stunning at the film's premiere," your line could be, "No one knows the red carpet like Nicole Kidman." If you add a "Right" or "Absolutely" (the YES) as an acknowledgment of what your co-host just said before you launch into your line—"And no one knows the red carpet like Nicole Kidman" (the AND)—it can make a huge difference in the segment looking like an actual conversation. It also creates relationship. I talk a little more about utters and mutters later in the book.

MEMORIZING YOUR CUES: A great way to stay engaged with your co-host is to memorize all of your cues (the thing that is said or something that happens right before your line that "cues" you to begin). This is true even if you are using a teleprompter. A cue is the verbal or physical reminder directly before your next action or line that reminds you that you are about to jump into action. If you memorize all of your cues, it will allow you to be with your co-host and the viewer, while creating a more natural-looking experience. Otherwise, you're more likely to be staring at your note cards, script, or the teleprompter more than necessary and deprive the viewer of a more engaging dynamic between you are your co-host.

STAY APPROPRIATE TO THE FORMAT: There are many areas of hosting that require a co-host. Oftentimes there will be some opportunity to banter with your co-host to create a fun, playful dynamic. Make sure you consider the type of show you are hosting and what is appropriate and not appropriate within that type of show. For example, you would not talk about getting drunk with your friends on a morning talk show format. But if you are auditioning for a more subversive type of show, like a late-night show, that type of anecdote might be appropriate and super funny.

PERCENTAGE OF TIME GIVEN TO CO-HOST V. CAMERA: Remember, this applies to co-hosting only, not interviewing. Interviewing is different. For co-hosting, you should be giving 65 to 70 percent of your attention to the camera and 30 to 35 percent of your attention to your co-host. This is both when you are talking and not talking. Pro tip: Try talking to your host while looking at the camera! Just give her a quick glance while talking to her, then spend the rest of the time looking at the camera. It may feel unnatural at first, but when you watch playback you'll realize that it can create a fun moment on screen where you are talking to your co-host but looking at us, the viewer.

DON'T FLIRT: Many co-hosting duos are male and female. Of course this rule applies to male/male and female/female as well. But don't flirt! You two are supposed to be a team and it's supposed to look like you have been working together for years. We don't want to see sexual chemistry. We want to see a fun, powerful duo that's having a good time. I have had clients and colleagues lose the opportunity for HUGE jobs when they displayed even a hint of flirting. This is especially true in more conservative areas of hosting, such as regional or national morning talk shows. You may think the extra wink or arm touch is going to seal the deal because you have chemistry. Instead it can really hurt you. So even if you do sense some chemistry with your co-host, don't let it create a less-than-professional dynamic.

MY COCKTAIL PARTY ANALOGY: Co-hosting is much like attending a dinner party with a friend that you recently shared a really fun experience with and being eager to tell your friends at the party all about it. When you see one of these friends, i.e., the audience, the two of you go back and forth sharing the story with the friend who wasn't there, each adding in your own elements of the story. The focus is on sharing the story with the friend, in the best, most fun way possible.

The good news is, if you go into TV hosting, there is a lot of work available. Keep in mind that as a host, you usually fall into one of two categories performance-wise: scripted and unscripted. Some hosts like super-scripted stuff and they like knowing what's going to happen, prepping it, and making sure they have clear map (infomercials, industrials, in-studio reporting, etc.). Some hosts like bullet points or a sketched-out idea of what needs to be accomplished and knowing what they have to get, but being able to do their own thing all the way through (morning show, shopping channels, a lot of reality TV). Don't worry—there are plenty of jobs for both these skill sets. But if you can DO BOTH, developing strengths in both these areas, you'll find many more doors opening for you as a host!

CHAPTER 3

THE BUSINESS OF HOSTING

So you want to start working as a host. Where do you start? Are you in a small market, or are you in a major market? Let's start with a smaller market approach and then we'll broaden our lens.

Smaller Market

Don't live in New York City or Los Angeles? Then you are not in a major market for TV hosts. I'm not saying you're not in a major city … Atlanta, Chicago, Boston, San Francisco are huge cities, but not for TV hosting work. You may be asking if you have to move to Los Angeles or New York City in order to make your dreams of hosting on-camera a reality. The answer is no, at least not immediately. One of the best plans of action for many hosts is to work a lot in smaller markets, get great footage for their reel and build up their résumé, and then come to a major market with the tools they need to start booking major jobs. When you start out in a major market, you can get the same thing accomplished, but you are dealing with SO much competition. You are going out against the best in the world right out of the gate. Starting in a smaller market will give you more opportunities because there are fewer people competing for those jobs, and it's a good place to learn the ins and outs, proper technique, lingo, and even the technical aspects of your business. Again, I'm not discouraging you from moving to LA or NYC … I'm just letting you know there is more than one way to accomplish your goal.

For example, I did a lot of work in San Diego and Orange County when I first moved to LA, because my parents lived in San Diego and I had a place to stay when I booked those jobs. Since there was far less competition, I booked on-camera jobs all the time. I used all that footage to create a great reel and had lots to put on my résumé. This put me in a better position to book work in LA … and it worked! Eventually, I was able to replace my San Diego hosting work with my Los Angeles hosting work on my reel and résumé. It was a great transition for me and it was nice to work doing what I loved, even if it wasn't in LA.

Host Tip: *It might be wise to plan a trip to LA or NYC to make sure you have stellar* *materials and will be ahead of the competition in your market. This is because these cities are on the cutting edge of what is trending in the industry. Shooting footage for your reel, taking a weekend hosting intensive workshop, and doing a headshot session in a city where most of the work is generated in this industry will put you ahead of your competition if you are working in a smaller market. It will also prepare you to hit the ground running if/when you decide to take the leap and move to a major market.*

HOW TO FIND JOBS: If you don't have an agent yet, you are probably wondering where you can even begin to find on-camera hosting work. Start with the following three items as a bare minimum to be considered for this type of work.

1. Headshot
2. Demo/Hosting Reel
3. Bio or Résumé

HEADSHOT: You will need to get professional hosting headshots taken by a professional photographer. This is super crucial. Your headshot should include professional hair and makeup, proper lighting, a jewel-toned wardrobe, and a "middle of the moment" smile.

Based on my own experience, and the comments I've heard from hosting agents and managers, a hosting headshot needs to feel a little more alive than the standard, static-smile commercial headshot. I call this the middle-of-the-moment shot. Imagine that you just heard something or are about to say something. Put yourself right smack dab in that middle-of-the-moment space, where you're alert and ready to respond, between "I heard you!" and "Wait 'til you hear this!" Also keep in mind that these photos need to show that you have the energy and power to carry a show. You need to have a strong presence. Own your space and show through these photos that you could have your own show. Stay away from low-energy, coy, or even bored-looking photos. We need to see that you have *the thing* that people want to watch!

Once you've nailed the moment, you'll have nailed the hosting headshot, too. Now go snap it and prepare to dazzle with some great pictures!

DEMO/HOSTING REEL: You have to have a hosting reel to get hosting work, which is different from the demo reel for experts as will be talked about in section two of this book. Repeat, you HAVE to have a hosting reel to get hosting work. It can be a general hosting reel or what we call an "expert reel." An expert reel also features you hosting, but where a general hosting reel will include many different areas of hosting (infomercial, industrial, entertainment, talk show, reality TV, man-on-the-street) with you talking on a myriad of topics, an expert reel is meant to highlight your particular area of expertise. So you may still have yourself doing an infomercial piece or a talk show piece, but everything in your reel will be you talking about your brand (sports, medicine, fashion, beauty, DIY, etc.). Expert reels have been growing in popularity the last couple of years as "general hosts," who used to stride the airwaves, slowly become extinct. Most hosts these days are either celebrities or experts ... this is true even with game shows! So if you are not yet a celebrity, it's great to have a general reel. But having an expert reel will almost certainly get you in more doors. Until this reel consists of paying jobs you've booked, you will have to shoot these pieces on your own.

To shoot pieces for your reel, there are a few options. One option is to contact your local public broadcasting network and find out if there is an opportunity to either audition or create content for their channel. A second option, if you want to do entertainment reporting, is to look up local film festivals at Withoutabox.com and contact a festival to get a press pass as a vlogger, which will allow you to interview actors and filmmakers on the red carpet. This is a great way to get footage, though you'll have to hire a camera operator with sound and rent a handheld mic for the event.

Another great way to get footage is to hire a shooter for the day. You can find one on Craigslist or Mandy.com. Then you can go out to a few locations (beach, park, street with some busy and hip shots) and get some fun exterior stand-ups (you standing up delivering a script/copy directly into the camera) or even some good man-on-the-street footage of you interviewing passersby. In post you can add some phone graphics and show titles to make it look really pro, like a fun digital series!

Host Tip: *Make sure you have a shooter with good sound equipment, including a lavalier microphone and a handheld mic. Good sound is important.*

Over the years, I have spoken to many agents and managers in Los Angeles about what they need to see in a hosting reel in order to consider a client. I've compiled the following list from their responses, and these items have become the must-haves in a hosting reel. This represents the major components representatives are looking for when considering new talent:

-INTRO AND OUTRO: These are stand-ups, where you're standing and talking directly into the camera. An intro is something like "Hello and welcome to Behind the Scenes" and an outro is something like "We had a great time today at Today's Buzz—see you next time."

-TOSSING: Tossing is a verbal communication exchange to redirect the viewer between two elements in a show format, such as B-roll, graphics, or another host. It is an important part of hosting and really good to put into your reel.

-CO-HOSTING: You definitely need a co-hosting segment in your reel where you are talking and interacting with another host. A lot of what hosts do is interact, so you need to show that you play well with others!

-DEMONSTRATION: You need to demonstrate something, whether it's how to cook something, how to wear something, or how to use a product; you need to be able to show that you can do something with your hands and talk at the same time.

-INTERVIEW: Even if you just do a man-on-the-street, where you grab a cameraperson, go out on the street, and ask a passerby a question (but always with the mic in your back/upstage hand). You can definitely talk to somebody you just met, but you need to conduct the exchange as an interview.

In general, your reel needs to be under two minutes. Remember, it's not a dramatic reel, so please put some fun music underneath it and make sure it moves at a nice pace. A montage at the beginning can work nicely, and make sure the clips are long enough that we can get a feel for you but short enough that we don't feel like we are watching an entire segment.

I know it might seem frustrating to go through this process, but it may lead to you being booked off of your reel without ever having to audition. It's heavenly!

-BIO/RÉSUMÉ: I'm including some samples of bios and résumés for you to use as a template in this book. A performance résumé, and you will see in the samples, look a bit different from the standard business résumé. For example, you often have your personal stats and union status listed at the top, and there are categories for what kind of performance experience you have had. Listing the cities where you've worked and what production companies/networks/directors you have worked with is way more important than a lengthy description of your job or how long you did the job. A section for special skills lets you pitch yourself by including all the specific skill sets that might qualify you for a job (being able to ride a horse, use a teleprompter, speak Russian, etc.).

TYLER BANKEN

HOST + ACTOR + DESIGNER

- social: @thetylerbanken

- height: 5'11"
- weight: 163

TV / FILM

• Wonderland	Supporting - Recurring	National
• Unbroken	Supporting	Global

HOSTING / LIVE EVENTS

• Urban Gardens	Show Host	Play Productions
• Think Outside: The Brand	Live Presenter - Recurring	Texas Tech University
• Imagine Lubbock Together	Live Event Speaker	Lubbock, TX

COMMERCIALS

• Walmart	Supporting	National
• Humira	Supporting	National
• Berkshire Hathaway	Supporting	Local
• Mercury Insurance	Supporting	Local
• Vodafone	Supporting	National
• Honda Private Jet	Supporting	Global
• Commonwealth Bank	Supporting	National

PRINT

• American Express	Model	National
• Chappy App	Model	National
• The Catalogue New Zealand	Model	International

TRAINING

• Masters in Landscape Architecture	Graduate School	Texas Tech University
• Commercial Audition Technique	Toby Lawless	Hollywood
• TV Hosting	Shannon O'Dowd	Hollywood

SPECIAL SKILLS

Landscape Architecture, TV Host, Live Presenter, Teleprompter Proficient, Golf, Cycle, Hiking, Swimming, Weight Training, Running, Loud Laugher, Superstar Beyonce Lip Syncer.

KELLEY BRUGGERE

Non-Union
Height 5'4" Weight 135lbs

HOSTING/SPOKESPERSON

Android TV	Entertainment News Host	Exo Level LLC
Arena Cinelounge	Red Carpet Host	Voltaire Media
Artisan Group	Show Host	SpyGame Studios
My Face My Body Awards	Show Host	GBK Productions
Van's Triple Crown of Surfing	Show Host	50Sense.com
The Movement	Host/Panelist	Inavision
Your Daily Checkup	Host	Inavision

PRODUCTION

Android TV	Producer	Exo Level LLC
"Keeper of the Cup" Movie	Producer	SpyGame Studios
Documentary TBD	Producer	Lunacy Productions

PRINT

DomPen	Model	DomPen.com
The Man's Shop	Model	The Gazette Times
"Princess Diana"	Model	The Oregonian
"Princess Diana"	Model	Portland Bridal
Mentor Graphics	Model	KVO Advertising

TRAINING

Commercial & Hosting Technique	Shannon O'Dowd	Culver City, CA
Advanced Hosting	Sena Series	Beverly Hills, CA
Shopping Network Hosting	Carolyne Barry	Los Angeles, CA
Advanced Hosting	Marki Costello	Los Angeles, CA
Actor's Improv	Bill Applebaum	Hollywood, CA
Lawless Commercial Casting Seminar	Toby Lawless	Hollywood, CA

SOCIAL MEDIA

Facebook: Kelley Bruggere
Instagram: @kelleybruggere
Twitter: @kelleybruggere

SPECIAL SKILLS: teleprompter, ear-prompter, writer/blogger, health, beauty & fitness advocate, world traveler, wine expert, competitive equestrian, BFA pursuer/painter, diver, dog lover, mother, happy breakfast cook.

There are places to find jobs in your city. Look at websites like Entertainment-Careers.net, TVJobs.com, Indeed, LinkedIn, and even Craigslist for places where you can start to find work. Keywords like TV Host, On-Air Host, Media Presenter, and Spokesperson are great to narrow down these types of jobs in your search.

Host Tip: *Only go to professional, staffed, official office spaces for auditions. Make sure someone knows where you are and all the contact and casting information you received from your point person. You can't be too careful!*

I have a few specific things you should keep in mind when starting to work on-camera and negotiating your own contracts before you have an agent or manager.

1. Usage
2. Usage
3. Usage

Seriously, this is everything. What is the usage of the spot? Where will it be airing? For how long? How long will they have the rights to your image? If it's going to be on broadcast TV, then you need to make more money. If they are going to be using it in multiple places (in-house, trade shows, TV broadcast, internet), then you definitely need to make more money. Be careful about the length of usage. Most companies will try to slide in usage in perpetuity if you don't know better. It's easier for them because they won't ever have to track it in the future. But do you really want someone to have the right to your image/likeness forever? If it's a product with a clear shelf life like a vacuum and they put out a new model every year, it might be okay. But I'd caution you against letting anybody use footage or photos of you for more than two years.

Major Market

All of the above information still applies if you live in the "major markets" for TV hosting, aka New York City or Los Angeles. I'd like to make a few additional recommendations, however, if you live in a land where hosts are flowing.

1. TAKE A HOSTING CLASS. In addition to learning the skills from this book, practice them in real time with someone where you can see yourself in playback. This is not only a great way to refine your skills on camera, but also to learn the little nuances of what works best in different areas of hosting. For example, some tonality of performing entertainment reporting copy is different than if you are performing industrial copy. Learning proper techniques for interviewing, co-hosting, and using a teleprompter will ensure you remain competitive. Even an ear-prompter is a great tool to have in your tool belt and can be very helpful on set when a teleprompter is either unavailable or technically not possible, or if you ever decide to get into narration/presenter work in the trade-show/convention world.

Good instructors will provide direction on your strengths, trends in the business, and more ways you can procure work. They can even recommend places where you can shoot footage for your reel, affordable editors who specialize in hosting demo reels, photographers who do great hosting headshots, etc. Also, agents and casting directors often turn to these instructors to find fresh talent, so it's great to be on their radar.

Last but not least, a hosting class is a great place to meet fellow aspiring hosts and begin building a community of help and support.

Here are some top coaches in Los Angeles and New York:

LOS ANGELES:

Shannon O'Dowd
Suzanne Sena
Marki Costello
Judy Jernudd

NEW YORK:

Mark Turner (also a hosting agent at Abrams Artists)
Leila Sbitani Hahn
Sean DeSimone (also the casting director for QVC)
Patricia Stark
Mary Mayotte

2. JOIN A FACEBOOK GROUP. The groups Hosts in LA and Hosts in New York are currently on Facebook. These are great communities where hosts can ask for advice, post their work, and find job postings. Hosting agents, managers, and casting directors are also members of these sites and post jobs here as well.

3. SELF-SUBMIT. If you live in NYC or LA, be sure to join these websites and set up profiles with two to five headshots, your performance résumé, and hosting reel so you can start self-submitting for jobs until you have a hosting agent.

- Actors Access: actorsaccess.com
- Casting Networks: castingnetworks.com
- Backstage West: backstage.com
- Casting Frontier: castingfrontier.com

Be sure to set up your account to have breakdowns submitted to you via email that match your profile so you can respond ASAP. Sometimes casting will only have these postings up for a few hours until they get the amount of submissions they need. Also, it's not advisable to do this unless you have a reel. Most of the time, it's a requirement to have a reel to book hosting work on these sites. Casting teams will often filter out the submissions that don't have reels attached, so there is a good chance your submission won't be seen if you don't have one up there.

There are occasionally no- or low-paying jobs that will take a chance on you as a new host. Especially since they aren't really paying. These can be great to get footage to build your reel! Make sure you have them sign something that states they will send you footage within ninety days. Otherwise, all that free work will be in vain. We don't want that!

4. TO JOIN OR NOT JOIN THE UNION. This is a sensitive topic. I know that all on-camera talent looks forward to the day that they can join the union. SAG/AFTRA membership is a validating step on many people's path to a performance career. The union is a great thing and does a lot of good, but remember the saying "Act in haste, repent in leisure." Once you join the union, you are no longer able to go out for any non-union work. Probably 90 percent of hosting work is non-union until you get to the point that you are a network host. Please think carefully before making this decision. Non-union work can be quite lucrative, especially in the Direct Response/Infomercial world. It also provides a great training ground for you to develop your skills until you are ready to compete against the major players who are in the union. Join too soon and you may find you are in over your head with the people that you are going up against for hosting roles. Also, there will be less work. Be thoughtful before making the leap with your union status.

Representation

Once you have a good hosting headshot, a bio/résumé, and a hosting reel, you're ready to find an agent. Contact your local SAG office to get a list of the SAG-franchised agencies in your area. Once you have that list, do a bit of research to see which of these agencies represent spokespeople and/or hosts. A great way to do this is to invest in an IMDbPro account, which allows you to get email addresses and direct contact information for all the agents at all the legitimate agencies. Their websites may have some of this information as well. Then you can send those agencies an email with a few paragraphs about you and your experience on camera, attach two to three headshots and your bio/résumé, and a link to your reel. Let them know you'd love the opportunity to meet with them to discuss the possibility of working together. In a week's time, follow up with a phone call or email if you haven't heard back. Closed mouths don't get fed!

Tim Kessler is one of the most respected managers in the business and his area of expertise is hosts. He was with a major agency in Los Angeles and after ten years, he branched out on his own. His advice to getting representation is to get your hosting demo reel on your own website or YouTube channel so that folks like him who pound the pavement on your behalf, or people who can actually hire you, have a place where they can find you.

Tim's advice: "A sizzle or a demo is a calling card and it's the most important piece of material that you can give your potential representation. It used to be a headshot and a resume was the most important thing."

He adds, "Eighty-five percent of auditions are Skype now. It used to be in the room, but that is less frequent. So you have to have a great sizzle/demo."

Finally, he stresses the need for the tape to be very specific:

"The tape should really talk about who you are, what your brand is, and how you act. After two minutes, if you still don't know who that person is, you're not going to want to represent them."

Hosting Agencies in Los Angeles: This is the list of agencies in LA that currently have a hosting or "alternative programming" division (meaning not scripted talent, like acting). You can get the current agent's contact info by getting an IMDb-Pro account. This list (and especially the agents) can fluctuate, so it's great to check those resources for the most current information.

I've included a template below to use when emailing agents that you might find helpful when you are ready to take this step. But please make sure you're ready!

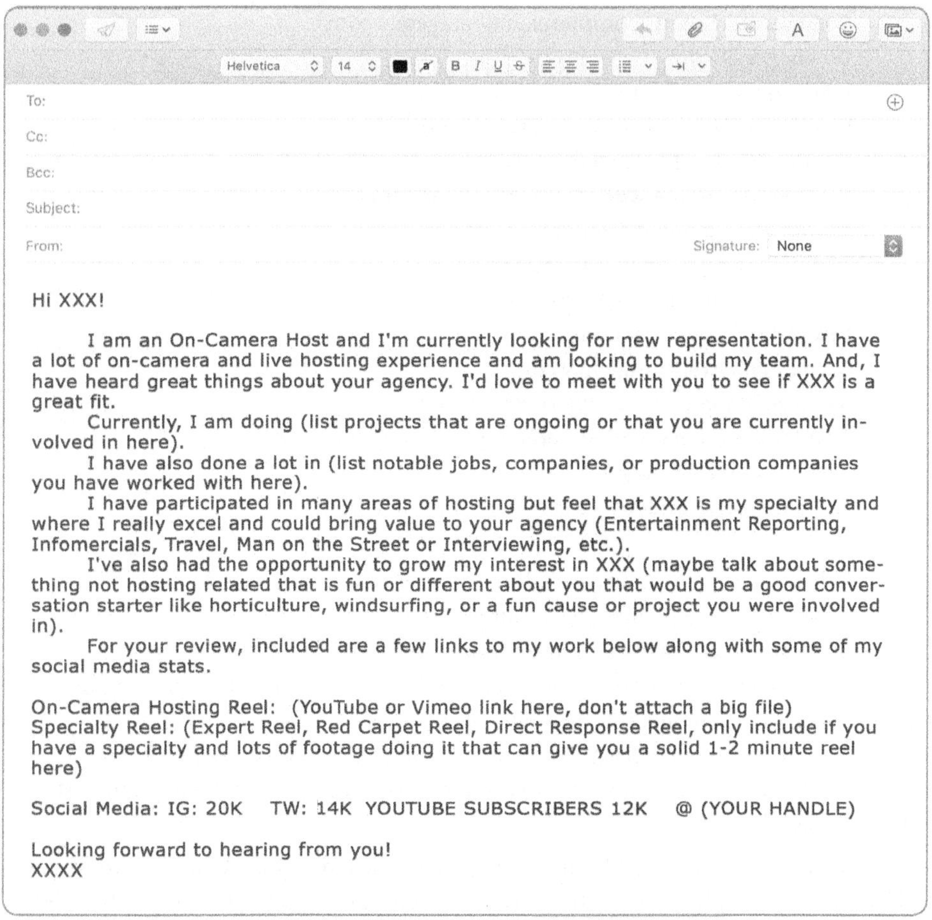

To:
Cc:
Bcc:
Subject:
From: Signature: None

Hi XXX!

I am an On-Camera Host and I'm currently looking for new representation. I have a lot of on-camera and live hosting experience and am looking to build my team. And, I have heard great things about your agency. I'd love to meet with you to see if XXX is a great fit.

Currently, I am doing (list projects that are ongoing or that you are currently involved in here).

I have also done a lot in (list notable jobs, companies, or production companies you have worked with here).

I have participated in many areas of hosting but feel that XXX is my specialty and where I really excel and could bring value to your agency (Entertainment Reporting, Infomercials, Travel, Man on the Street or Interviewing, etc.).

I've also had the opportunity to grow my interest in XXX (maybe talk about something not hosting related that is fun or different about you that would be a good conversation starter like horticulture, windsurfing, or a fun cause or project you were involved in).

For your review, included are a few links to my work below along with some of my social media stats.

On-Camera Hosting Reel: (YouTube or Vimeo link here, don't attach a big file)
Specialty Reel: (Expert Reel, Red Carpet Reel, Direct Response Reel, only include if you have a specialty and lots of footage doing it that can give you a solid 1-2 minute reel here)

Social Media: IG: 20K TW: 14K YOUTUBE SUBSCRIBERS 12K @ (YOUR HANDLE)

Looking forward to hearing from you!
XXXX

Have some legit jobs under your belt before self-submitting, a great headshot, a strong bio or resume, and a good reel.

(Attach 2-3 professional hosting headshots with different looks, your resume or bio)

Hosting Agency/Manager List (mostly LA based):

CESD: CESDTalent.com
Abrams Artists : abramsartists.com
Agency for the Performing Arts: apa-agency.com/
AKA Talent Agency: akatalent.com
Bobby Ball Talent Agency: bbatalent.com
Buchwald Agency: buchwald.com
CAA: caa.com
CMEG: cmeg.com
Commercial Talent: commercialtalentagency.com
Gersh: gersh.com
ICM: icmpartners.com
Innovative Artists: innovativeartists.com
Kaplan Stahler: kaplanstahler.com
Ken Lindner and Associates: kenlindner.com
Napoli Management Group: tvtalent.com
NTA Talent Agency: ntatalent.com
Paradigm: paradigmagency.com
SBV Talent: sbvtalent.com
Stone Manners: smsagency.com
Synergy Management: synergytalent.net
TKO Media (management company): tkomediainc.com
United Talent Agency: unitedtalent.com
William Morris/Endeavor: wmeentertainment.com

When sending in your materials to these agents via email, make sure to include:

1 Two to three paragraphs about your background

2 Highlights of what you have done in the hosting space

3 Your area of preference or where you've found the most success in hosting (entertainment reporting, infomercials, etc.)

4 Two to three headshots of yourself along with a bio or résumé

5 Where you see yourself providing the most value in the agency, and last but not least …

6 The best way to get hold of you to schedule a meeting. Make sure to include your email, phone, website (if you have one), and link to your reel in the body of the email.

Host Tip: *Don't attach a QuickTime or MP4 file to your submission email. This will make your email too large, which means risking that it won't go through because of its size, will be sent to spam, or will be deleted because the recipient is annoyed at being sent such a large file. No better way to start off on the wrong foot with the agent!*

Plan on following up in one week with a phone call or email (phone call is better) to make sure they received your materials. After that, don't bug them again. If they don't respond to two attempts to contact them, they are probably not interested right now. But they may be in the future, so best not to look like a pest and leave a bad impression. I'd say submitting to an agency every six months is a good schedule. Try to have something fresh of note to add if you are resubmitting. Something like "I just booked the Flashy Lashes hosting job and added a piece from it to my reel. Would love for you to check it out!"

Lastly, you can always mail a hard copy of your materials. Many agencies will say that is the preferred/only way they accept talent submissions. I find that in today's era of technology, and because hosts must have a reel to be considered by a hosting/alternative programming agent, sending an email is the easiest and best way to submit. Whatever route you choose, make sure you research what the agency says on their website about their recommendation for submissions.

Licensing

Today's individual image can be someone's business, brand, and livelihood. Look at action figures from the Marvel or Stars Wars franchises, or even public figures like the Kardashians who get huge paychecks from just holding a product in an Instagram post. Someone's image or likeness can be a powerful tool used by brands and advertisers to hit the emotions of their consumers and convince them to make a purchase. Where does the line of what constitutes your image or likeness begin and end?

We can understand why the actress from the Phillips commercials sued Bayer for using a bobblehead as her replacement. Without knowing the full terms of her agreement with Bayer, it's safe to say that they agreed to compensate her an established amount for the use of her image/likeness. Once they decided to terminate the use of her physical image, they continued to use a bobblehead of her. Is using a bobblehead of her the same as using her image? And is it legally permissible?

As someone who also has her own bobblehead as the spokesperson for Cable One, I know that I had to take a look at my own negotiations about how my image would be used. I have given them rights to my image and likeness through the extent of my contract. But would that include the use of my bobblehead after my contract expires?

That's kind of a gray area ... for me, and for the Phillips actress as well. In my situation, I don't think they would try to use any version of my likeness without compensating me. But *could they* without legal ramifications? It's possible. Which is what makes this story and case so interesting.

For me as a corporate spokesperson, and for so many actors, actresses, hosts, and others in the media, there is a need for some legal clarity around the issue of what constitutes a person's likeness. Especially in this age of technology and social media, where the parameters of how someone's personal brand can be used to sell a product, some additional protections need to be defined.

Don't let anyone tell you this is an issue of greed on the talent's part. It's not. Actors, hosts, and performers have every right to be compensated well if their image is used to generate income for a company or brand. It's also important to recognize that use of your image can overexpose you in that role (or category of products) and make it harder to get more work. For example, if you were highly recognizable as the hero talent in a Bissell vacuum commercial that ran like gangbusters for a year, other companies like Dirt Devil or Shark wouldn't touch you for five to ten years since your image is associated with another product and company.

If you are like me and have been the face of a major cable, internet, and home phone company for over six years, you will never in the foreseeable future be considered as the next company spokesperson for Spectrum, DirecTV, or Cox unless they pulled a "Paul from Verizon" campaign like Sprint did. (Wink wink, I'm talking to you, DirecTV.)

As you can see, we have to be paid well because this is what we do for a living and once we're overexposed, it limits what we can do. For example, can you see Stephanie Courtney being the face of anything else in the near future besides being the Progressive girl? Of course not. Does she get paid handsomely to the tune of one to two million dollars a year for that gig? Yes, she does. She is truly part of that company's brand and has brought them so much success. People know her, they remember the spots that she does, and when they look for insurance, they think of Progressive. To me, that girl is doing her job and deserves every penny she makes.

Where does license permission begin and end? With the internet today in addition to mass television media, this is a larger discussion that all actors and spokespeople need to look at. We need to be paying attention, to be educated, and to have our representation fighting for our rights in this space.

CHAPTER 4

ON-CAMERA TECHNIQUE

Whenever you're auditioning for a hosting job, there are a few areas you need to have totally locked down in order to make a powerful connection with the camera. Those areas are:

1. The first line of the script copy
2. The last line
3. The name of the show or product
4. Any names of important people mentioned in the copy
5. YOUR name

Often when you are being auditioned or tested for hosting jobs, you'll be told by someone trying to be helpful that you don't have to worry about memorizing the script, "just be familiar with the copy." That may be true. However, if you want to make a solid impression with casting and the producers, I'd strongly suggest being very familiar with the areas mentioned above.

PRO TIPS FOR LANDING THE JOB!

1. Eye Contact: As a host, we are supposed to deliver information into the camera. That's kind of the major thing we do! However, it is a common misconception when auditioning that you should look into the camera the entire time. This will read as completely unnatural. When you are hosting, you are being yourself, sharing an event, product, etc. We want to have a believable experience of you, as if you were speaking to us in real life. So let me ask you, how often do you talk to people and just stare at them? Think about it ... NEVER! People don't do that. They occasionally will take a glance around to gather their thoughts. If someone just stared at you the whole time, you'd most likely freak out. The same is true when you're on camera. Giving your audience an occasional break in eye contact with the camera will be calming to us as the viewer. Just as it is in real life.

2 Using Your Environment: This tip piggybacks on the point above and actually adds another level. When you are on location for a hosting job (or even if you are simply auditioning/testing and the audition copy has you on location), it can be super powerful to create your environment by looking around in the first ten seconds or so of the read to show us that you are actually someplace in the world ... even if you're simply in an audition room or studio. If it's an audition, it adds another layer to the read and allows us to feel like we are there with you. Take the line "I'm at the base of the most active volcano on all of the Hawaiian Islands." If you take a second to look around and up while you are delivering that first line, it brings the audience to the base of the volcano with you. It doesn't matter if it's an audition in front of a blank wall; our brain will start to see the volcanic rock and ash around you. The human brain's capacity for imagination is amazing. Take advantage of it!

3 What to Do with Your Hands: Be sure to have your hands "in the world" of the frame the entire time you are on camera. A good way to do this is to have the hands loosely clasped, crossed over each other (bunny hands), or in a diamond shape (my least favorite, but an option). You mostly just want to leave your hands in a good resting position, one you can adjust whenever necessary. You're usually framed from the waist up, or with three quarters of your body in frame. Having your hands resting right around your belly button allows for them to be in frame the whole time. That positions them to make gestures within the frame. If your hands start down by your sides, that often means you'll be bringing them continually in and out of frame as you make natural gestures, which can be visually disruptive and a jarring experience for viewers. Also be mindful of not making many gestures too close to your face. That can be incredibly distracting as well to your audience. Lastly, try to avoid using repetitive hand gestures that can start to look like a tic. Whatever you do with your hands, definitely don't point your finger at us! People don't like to be pointed at … in life, and definitely not on camera. That's why you often see political candidates during speeches do what would be a point, but their pointer finger is tucked in, not extended out. They have been trained not to point during

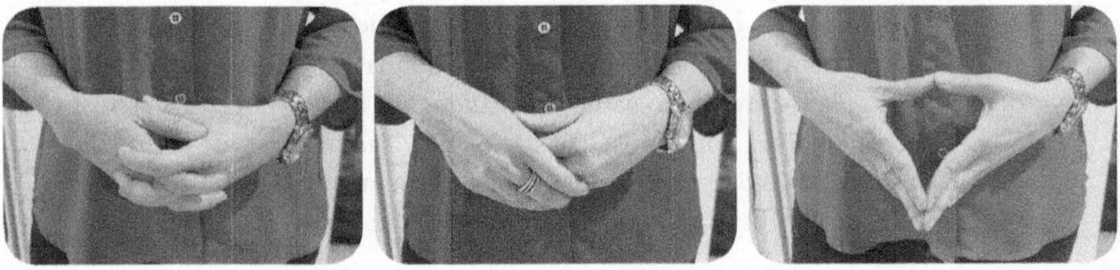

their speeches! The same is true for us as hosts. Again, keep your hands in frame, be mindful of repetitive hand gestures, stay away from too many movements close to your face, and don't point at us!

4. The Power of "Utters & Mutters": One of my mentors, (and a dear friend) Carolyne Barry, taught me the power of "utters and mutters," and it was a game changer for me in my career. Let's first define the term. "Utters and mutters" refer to those single words or sounds that you can put anywhere into your scripted copy to make it your own. Even if you've been instructed to stay on script for your appearance and avoid any unscripted banter, you can always do an utter or mutter. This can mean a difference as minimal as the one between "Las Vegas has become the hottest place on the planet for amazing restaurants" and the uttered and muttered version "Now, Las Vegas has become the hottest place on the planet for amazing restaurants. Mmmm!" You have not changed the script. You've just added a word or sound to connect it more to you in the moment. But here is the trick: you can't pre-plan these moments. My recommendation is, once you get your script, put five to ten in your back pocket that feel inspirational and appropriate to the content at hand. Please don't choose and place them in your script in advance, otherwise they will become a schtick and actually hurt you in an audition. Not only will they lose their spontaneity (the whole reason for them!), it will look like you are a Johnny One Note only capable of pre-planning one fun choice. If you make a different choice with your utter or mutter every time, that's when they have magical power. Trust me, they can be MAGIC!

As hosts, we are not just reporters. Yes, we are often providing information that could sometimes be seen as news. But we are more than that. We are a vessel for providing our audience with an experience by giving them access to people, products, and information that can be educational, entertaining, and even transformative. Of course, we also have to be engaging throughout that process. We aren't just "presenting" information. The goal is to give the viewer an authentic experience of YOU while still delivering the copy or communicating the information required for the segment or spot. So … you must have opinions. This doesn't mean changing the words. This means that we need to understand how you feel about what you are saying, by the way you say them. We need to know if you are excited, perplexed, intrigued, inquisitive, or even playfully frustrated. We want to have an experience of you and feel like we are getting to know you. Your job is to communicate the information while simultaneously creating a relationship with your viewers. That can only be done if we get to see who you are, which can be done by the way you say things and what makes you tick!

Host Tip: *I recommend never going more negative than playful frustration, which means being slightly annoyed but still having a sense of humor about it, unless you are doing a rant piece. It's too dangerous and can backfire on you by making you look unlikable.*

Teleprompter

Most of my clients approach their initial use of a teleprompter with a mixture of intimidation and fear. They're falling victim to a wide range of worries. *What if the words scroll too fast? What if no words appear at all? What if I suddenly have a brain fart and forget how to read?!* When my clients are experiencing any of these fears, I remind them to take a few deep, sloooooow breaths and remember this old chestnut (which applies equally to teleprompters and life in general): worrying is just praying for what you don't want. Turns out Bobby McFerrin had it right when he sang, "Don't worry, be happy!" Then I lay the truth on them: teleprompters will actually make their jobs much easier, and their performances on screen so much simpler to accomplish. When approaching teleprompters properly, you won't even have to worry about what you're saying. You just need to be present in the moment and use the words you're being prompted to say in a believable and enthusiastic way.

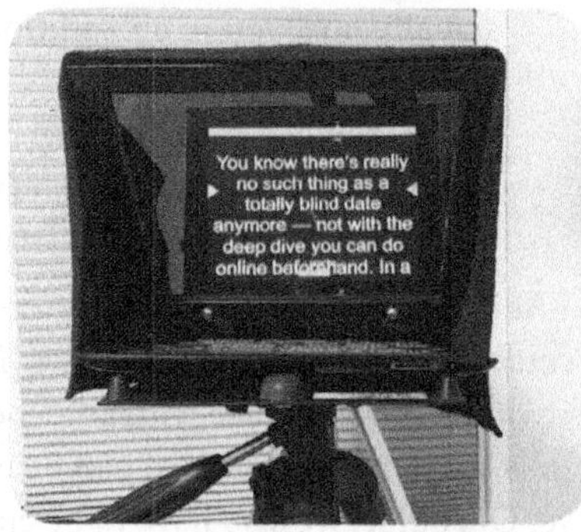

The first thing that I want to assure you about teleprompters is that you are always in control. You will have a teleprompter operator assigned to you on the day of set and it is his or her job to follow your pacing, your energy, and your speed … it is never the other way around. You don't adjust to them; they adjust to you. You speed up, they speed up … you slow down, they slow down … you stop, they stop. It really is a beautiful thing!

The other thing you have control over is the font size. Please keep in mind that every prompter is different, so you can't say, "Give me Times New Roman font size 12" and the prompter operator will know what you mean. You have to start at a certain font size and just let the operator know if you want to go larger or smaller.

I recommend going as small as you possibly can while still being able to comfortably read the copy. The reason I say this is that if the font is too big, only a few words will fit on the screen at a time, making it more difficult to understand the full concept of what you're saying. Another cool thing our brain can do while reading and having more words available is it can actually grab context! The more words you have on the screen at one time, the more your brain can understand and grasp the concept of what you're saying, even before it hits you on a conscious level. If you have the font too big, the words can break into the next line, and there may be too few words on the screen for you to capture the concept. So, again, go as small with the font size as you can while still being comfortable.

I highly encourage you to find your prompter operator *as soon as you get to set* and introduce yourself. I would then ask the person to run through the script with you on the prompter. For one thing, this will give you an opportunity to make sure the script you have been given matches the one that the operator is using. Sometimes the wrong script has been loaded into the prompter, and it's super important to find that out before you start shooting. This is also a great way to ensure that if there are grammatical errors in the script, you fix them now, so once shooting it doesn't look like you were saying things incorrectly.

Checking in with the operator will also allow you to mark the areas in the script you would like to emphasize, and see if any adjustments need to be made. You can usually have the option of making things bold, italicizing or underlining them, or even changing the color. Also, you might want to put concepts, names of places, or ideas in quotation marks in order to emphasize them appropriately when they appear on the prompter.

I've also had clients save themselves by making sure that hard-to-pronounce last names or products' pronunciations are spelled out phonetically so they wouldn't be at risk of saying them incorrectly. Then there are the times you need to say something like "nine-one-one" instead of "nine-eleven" … written numerically the same, but obviously with very different meanings. In this case, you might suggest spelling part of the number out, or putting it in digits. Whatever will make it easier for your brain to process in the moment on camera.

Last but not least, when you huddle on set with the prompter operator while the crew is still setting up the shots and lighting, it is the mark of a true professional. You are telling the crew, producer, director, and client that you value their time and that once shooting begins, you will be truly prepared and ready. It's a great way to get hired again!

I would recommend always keeping your eyes close to the eye-line marker on the teleprompter screen. This makes it look like you're genuinely looking down the barrel of the lens and appears way more natural to your audience. Try implementing some slight, casual head motions and occasional eye pop (widening your eyes a bit for emphasis) from time to time to mask your eyes' back-and-forth reading.

Working with a product and using a prompter can be really tricky, especially if you are supposed to stay relatively close to the script. When you're given the freedom to banter (say your own thing) while working with a product, it makes things a lot easier. For example, one of my clients is a chef. He is amazing on network shows, running through his recipes while being super charismatic and fun. But making a meal while having to say exactly what was on the prompter was super challenging for him, understandably so. How do you look down at your dish or show how a pan works while looking at the camera? Good question. Here are a few tips!

1. One, memorize all your cues. Go through the script in advance and mark all the areas where you will need to look down. Memorize the three or four words before that moment (cue) and then figure out if you can take a beat to look down, or if you need to memorize the following line where you are doing the action so you don't have to look into the prompter and deliver the line while doing the action naturally.
2. Try throwing in an utter and mutter to fill the space while you are performing the action.
3. Grab larger chunks from the prompter before delivering your lines, then do a conversational look up in the middle of the line to grab your next chunk. People do this all the time when they are talking and it comes off very naturally.

There is a fine art to co-hosting, which we covered earlier in the book. However, there is a separate but equal art to co-hosting with a prompter. Remember that co-hosting needs to be a conversation. If you are looking at the prompter the whole time and never at your co-host, that's hardly a conversation. A great way to tackle co-hosting with a prompter is to memorize your cues, as we discussed while working with a product. Memorize the three words that your co-host says at the end of his last line that leads into your line. If you have those memorized, you get to be present with your co-host, listen and acknowledge, and stay in the world of the segment until you hear those three words. Once you hear them, you'll know to go back to the prompter and start reading and performing your portion again.

I'd also like to add that a lot of my clients ask about the free prompter programs that you can find online. I really caution against using these to learn teleprompter. They are all self-paced, so your read follows whatever speed that prompter program is set at, not the other way around. This is never the way it's going to be on an actual set, so you want to be very careful using programs where you're not following your own natural speed, cadence, and rhythm. If you are going to use a prompter app, I'd recommend something like PromptSmart that follows your voice, or iCUE that uses your phone like a remote to the tablet, so the pacing can be controlled.

Wired Ear-Prompter

Ear-prompter proficiency is a great skill to have as a host, even though you don't see them being used as much on sets these days. Of course, there are still IFBs (which stands for either "interrupt for broadcast" or "interruptible feedback/foldback" depending on who in the industry you are asking), the inner-ear devices that allow producers or directors to communicate with on-air talent while they are on camera.

Ear-prompters are different from IFB inner-ear devices, though to the untrained eye they look very much the same. An ear-prompter is actually an inner-ear device that is plugged into a recorder and plays back a tape of your own voice. Using an ear-prompter begins with you recording the script into the recording device (like you do with voice memos to remind yourself what to get at Trader Joe's). You then plug in the inner-ear device and play your own recording back to yourself as you talk about four words behind yourself. Yes, it is a little weird listening to yourself and speaking what you hear at the same time. Not an easy skill, but once you have it, you have it. It's kind of like riding a bike. And like riding a bike or any skill, some people pick it up faster than others.

Below are some basic techniques, as well as the equipment you can buy to install an ear-prompter setup at home and start practicing.

There are wired ear-prompters and wireless ear-prompter earpieces. There are recorders that are old-school tape recorders, which some prefer because they are easy to pause and rewind slightly during a performance. Another advantage of a tape recorder is that you can fast-forward to a specific place and re-record from there if only part of the script changes. With digital, that is not a possibility.

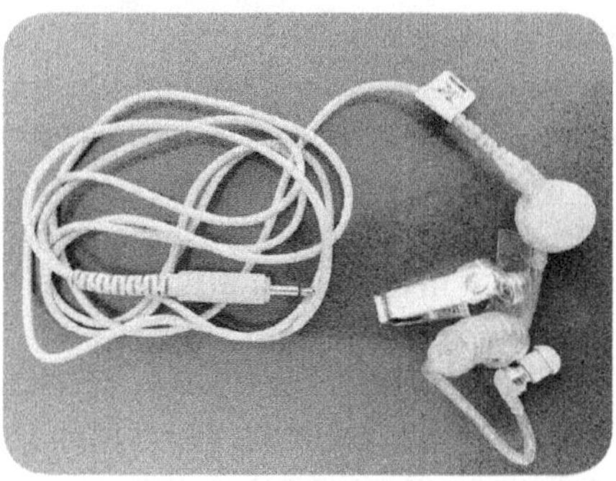

I personally do not want to mess with my prompter once I start using it, so I prefer using the digital recorders, even if it means having to reload or re-record my script from the beginning if there's a change. The other downside to a tape recorder device is that they don't make them anymore. If you are using one, it's either old, refurbished, or has been sitting on a shelf for a long time. The chances of it breaking during a gig, or heaven forbid a performance, feels too high for me to risk. That being said, I still know a lot of seasoned presenters who only use the tape recorders, so you can decide what is best for you.

Here is the 411 on loading and performing a script with an ear-prompter:

1 Make sure nothing is plugged into the recorder. This might seem obvious, but if the earpiece is plugged in while you are recording, either you will not have sound or it will sound muffled.

2 Don't hold the recorder too close to your mouth. Hold it about six or eight inches from your mouth at chin height, with the recorder in horizontal position (not vertical facing you, as this increases the chances of picking up lip-smacking and mouth noise).

3 Give yourself time to settle. Countdown, three-two-one, out loud before beginning to read your copy. This gives you time once you press play to put the recorder back in a hidden place during your performance (you need more time for a live show, because you also may have to cue media or turn on your mic).

4 Read more slowly than normal. Read the script about 15 to 20 percent slower than you would normally perform it. You may have to adjust this later once you start performing and see if it needs to be a hair faster or slower, but slowing down by 15 to 20 percent is a good place to start.

5 Read the script without inflection. Reading without inflection allows you to put your own spin on it in the moment. If you load your script into the prompter with a specific tone or performance, you will be locked into that way of doing it.

6 Make a noticeable noise for cues. If you have a PowerPoint presentation and need to cue yourself to change slides, or to remind yourself to take a certain action in a script (turn something on, gesture to something, etc.), make sure to drop in a verbal cue you are going to notice. Words like "beep," "ding," and "click" are great options. Also words like "beat" or "pause" are good to put in during a transition. You can even give yourself directions like "point," "sit," and "start." The key is to say these cues in a recognizably different tone of voice. If it is loaded into your recorder in the same tone in which you are delivering your script, you may wind up saying the word before your brain realizes it's a direction and not something in the script. You'll be saying your directions to yourself out loud! Going in a really low or really high pitch or just using a silly voice or tone accentuates those directions so your brain will hear them as unique from the script, which in turn will prompt you to take the appropriate action.

7 Barbie and Ken Scripts. This is a term in the convention and trade-show industry for a co-hosted script, most often delivered by a man and woman.

Hence the term "Barbie and Ken." When you are doing a co-hosted script, sit side by side with your co-host and record together with both recorders equidistant from both of your mouths at that six-or-eight-inch mark away from your chin. Do the countdown together, and then each read the lines while both recorders are recording simultaneously. This will ensure you have the same timing for your performance. This technique can be used in a pre-tape situation where teleprompter or cue cards won't work but you have to stay on script, like an infomercial or industrial (a video that is to be housed internally for a company) where everything said has to have been approved by a legal department so you don't accidentally make false claims.

8 Another great thing to consider when using an ear-prompter is using an earplug in the ear that doesn't have the prompter in it. You may be performing in a noisy venue, so drowning out noise around you is really important to make it easier to hear your prompter. It's also tiring for the brain to struggle to make out the words. I recommend ear plugs even on a quiet set, because I think creating an environment where all you hear is the recording is easiest. I even know some performers who use the earpiece in both ears (what we call in the business going "in-stereo" with our prompter) because they feel that they get less tired and it's less work for their brain when both ears are hearing the script instead of just one.

9 Wear clothes that allow you to place your ear-prompter recorder somewhere. There are thigh and waist straps on the market for ladies that have a place to slide the recorder, so that's an option. Sometimes just wearing a blazer that has inside pocket or slacks with a back pocket is the easiest way to go. Men don't typically have trouble with this, as most of their pants have pockets and their jackets have inside pockets, but it's still worth noting. The goal is to make the prompter setup as unnoticeable as possible. If you are using a wired earpiece, run the wire down your back, under your clothing, and have it come out your shirt and go into your back pocket or inside jacket pocket. We don't want the audience to see how the magic is made!

10 You will often get a bump in pay for providing your own prompter kit. This can be anywhere from $50 to $250, depending on the job. Have extra batteries, a backup recorder, and an additional headset. Things break, and you don't want that to happen on set. Especially if you have been paid for providing that service.

Enunciation Exercises

Peter Piper picked a peck of pickled peppers.
How many pecks of pickled peppers did Peter Piper pick?
If Peter Piper picked a peck of pickled peppers,
Where's the peck of pickled peppers Peter Piper picked?

Sally sells seashells by the seashore.
The shells she sells are surely seashells.
So if she sells shells on the seashore,
I'm sure she sells seashore shells.

Red leather, yellow leather.
(My favorite! Works out all the areas of the mouth and easy to do in a pinch!)

How much wood would a woodchuck chuck
If a woodchuck could chuck wood?
He would chuck, he would, as much as he could,
And chuck as much as a woodchuck would
If a woodchuck could chuck wood.

CHAPTER 5

THE AUDITION ROOM

The audition room can be a daunting place unless you know how to be prepared for it. If you see a tricky word that you know is going to be a roadblock in your audition script, try creating some space in front of it or behind it so that your body and mind can prepare for it. For example, an entertainment script I was helping a client prepare recently had the phrase "this introspective, highly respected actor." The words "introspective" and "highly respected" are not easy to say right after each other. So, if you are saying a word, phrase, or someone's name and you keep having challenges with it, give yourself a mini pause right before you say it. For the example I just gave you, I might say "this introspective (pause) highly respected actor." It does wonders, and no one will notice.

Some other good ideas are to change the spelling of the word to a phonetic spelling or hyphenate the word so your brain can make sense of it. Then, if you are still having trouble, change the word to a synonym. There is no reason to lose the job over a word. If you can't get past it, change it to set yourself up for success. Otherwise, you'll be in your head, afraid of the word during the whole read, and you won't be present and available during the audition.

If you are auditioning, there are three scenarios for where the audition copy will be: on 1) a board, similar to a cue card (a nightmare when you are supposed to be delivering into camera), 2) a teleprompter (this happens when all the angels are singing and the stars align), or 3) a piece of paper in your hand.

When you find out there is a board and you happen to not have the copy memorized, you need to take a few minutes and get it as memorized as best you can. Even if that means letting the person running the sign-ups know that you need some additional time and to call in a person or two after you. Take the time! Being memorized or almost memorized is going to serve you so much better than having to continue to break your contact with the camera, look over at the board, find your place with someone else's probably terrible handwriting, and come back to the camera. Avoid it if at all possible.

The most doable audition scenario for a host or spokesperson (when a teleprompter is not available) is when they let you hold the script or audition copy. In this situation, the script is to be folded in half (if possible; it cuts down on the paper shaking if you are nervous), you should put your elbow against your torso where it would naturally land, your arm and hand are at a 90-degree angle from your body, and you should have the script directly below your eyes with the paper straight out. This way it's not in front of your face to the side, where you have to take time to pull it back in front of your eyes and find your place every time, or being waved around and distracting from your performance. Eventually when you get stronger at auditioning, this doesn't have to be quite so strict. But it's helpful when you are first starting.

If you need to look down at your script, don't sweat it! The time you spend peeking at your script might feel like an eternity to you, but it's just milliseconds to the casting person or producer watching you. It's so much better to take that extra second to grab the next part of your copy than to struggle to remember it. Remember, we'll see that struggle in the camera. Your expression will have a "deer in the headlights" look. Not what we want to project in an audition!

Go ahead and look down. When you do, try and grab phrases. Like I said, if it takes a second (or even two or three), that's okay. Casting and the producers don't expect you to have everything memorized. Just own it. Own the space, own the time. I promise, it isn't nearly as long as you think it is.

A phrase you'll often hear from casting directors or producers is "make it your own." The term means that you have permission to add a little bit here and there, aka "banter" (not to mention those old pals, utters and mutters), to make the script feel natural for you.

This is actually to get around a SAG union rule that you can't have actors write content without compensating them. Instead of telling you to come up with your own wording in the given scenario, they tell you to "make it your own," implying that you are personalizing it to enhance your own performance and not actually writing copy for them. Even though there will be times they end up using what an actor or host comes up with in the room in the actual spot that airs.

Now if you are told to stick more closely to the script, adding those utters and mutters is still something you can do that won't really change the script. Adding a "now," "wow," "so," "okay," "amazing," or even a "hmm," "yum," or "mm-hmm" doesn't really change the script and actually infuses YOU and YOUR PERSONALITY into the audition copy, which will make your performance stand out from the crowd. Saying "Look at those high heels and stilettos" versus adding "Wow, look at those high heels and stilettos" can make a big difference in your read. More often than not, the casting person won't even realize you added a word, she will just think you were great and had tons of personality!

Remember, the entire goal is to have YOU be YOU through saying the lines. This is Hosting 101 through graduation!

I always say if you make a mistake in the first 20 percent of the copy, own it and say, "I'd like to do that again." Don't ask and apologize profusely, just start again ... because you're going to be in your head the whole time if you try to keep going. You are going to remember that mistake and it will most likely color the rest of your performance. Alternatively, if you're about 75 percent into the audition and you make a mistake or mess up a word, make it a "beautiful mistake," which means you make it work and keep going. Because you don't want to say at that point, "I need to start again from the beginning." Especially if casting has a room full of people waiting to audition and you were doing great up until that point. Making the mistake work is human ... people mess up when they are speaking all the time. This is the same for hosts on national TV. It's the mark of a true professional to make the mistake work for you and keep going. It can be a funny, memorable moment that might even help you get the job!

It's crucial to handle lists appropriately in an audition. It could be lists of places, lists of stars in a movie, lists of the best foods at a hot restaurant, lists of all the wonderful things a product can do for you. Whatever the case may be, make sure you either 1) have your list build with excitement/enthusiasm or 2) give each item in your list a different flavor, tone, or color. It's important that each item stand out on its own.

10 Audition Pointers When You Get Your Script:

1. Read through your script a few times full voice without inflection to get it into your body.
2. Make sure you memorize the first and last line of the script as well as the show name. At the very least, those things (including your name) need to be delivered into camera, without requiring you to look at your sides/copy.
3. Determine what makes this show or subject more distinctive, interesting, or fun than other shows that cover similar territory. If it's a product or service, think about how it will make the viewer's life more affordable, fun, easier, or better. Underline those things so you remember to give them more energy and emphasis.
4. Make sure to give a little extra emphasis to the show or product name, your name, and anyone else's name that appears in the copy/sides. They need extra power and energy from you as well.
5. If you ask a question in the copy, make it a real question! You should look like you want to know the answer as badly as the audience does.
6. When you get to the end of the script, deliver it like an end. Even if you are "tossing" (passing the segment) to another host, a package, or a commercial, you want the handoff to be smooth and powerful.
7. If you are listing things in your script, make each thing you list different.

My two easy ways to do this are to either make the list build, or give each thing on the list a different inflection or color so it lives on its own and the list doesn't just start to all run together in the viewer's mind.

8 If you are at a location in the script, take a beat when you are talking about being in that place and look around for a second to take in your environment. "Hello, I'm XXX and we are at the Aztec ruins ..." If you take a second to acknowledge that you are at a place with your eye-line (i.e., look around), it will transport us there too and we will feel like you are in that place.

9 Don't get bogged down with punctuation or paragraph breaks. Those are in there because the script has to be written that way. Just because there is a period doesn't mean you have to pause. Just because there is a new paragraph doesn't mean you have to give a longer pause. Throw all that away. We don't always talk with punctuation, so you just need to read the script in a way that registers as natural and compelling.

10 Be prepared! If there is ANYTHING in the copy you don't know ... how to pronounce something, someone's name, the history of what you are talking about, who someone is, etc. ... look it up! Set yourself up for success and it will not only prepare you for the audition, it will put you ahead of the competition.

These are a few great insider tips to help you really stand out in your auditions and bring your authentic you forward, along with incorporating good on-camera technique. If you give these a try, you'll see a shift in your auditions and bookings for sure.

We can often feel as talent that casting directors are these terrifying figures that will either open or shut the door for opportunity in our quest to realize our on-camera careers. We can feel quite intimidated by them, seeing them as gatekeepers who will keep us from entering the magical world of getting to be on-camera talent, and fear that they could potentially squash our on-camera dreams. However, what I have found from being in this business long enough is that although casting directors are a necessary filter between all the talent in the world and the jobs available (as well as producers and networks that are looking to find the right people for them), we often give them more power over us than is healthy or helpful when going into audition rooms.

The truth is, casting directors have a job to do and a role to fill. They have been given the responsibility to learn what a client, producer, network, or studio wants to see for a particular on-camera job and to deliver the absolute best (as well as a healthy range) of people who could possibly fit that role. There are three things a casting director wants from you. They are:

1 Don't make them look bad.
2 Be who you say you are.
3 Solve their problem.

1 Don't make them look bad.

I know it seems so simple, but this is really the truth. Their jobs (and careers) are contingent upon being able to consistently deliver quality options to their clients. If you go into the room and do a great job, act professionally, show up on time, and do your best to deliver the performance in the way you were directed to, the casting director is a very happy camper.

2 Be who you say you are.

This may sound ridiculously simple, but it can really be upsetting for casting, especially if they only bring in a limited number of people, for you to misrepresent yourself. Sometimes they are looking for a very specific thing, and if you come in differently than the way you are advertised online, that can be a big problem. If all your shots are of you with long blond hair and you show up with a black bob, are twenty years older, or are thirty pounds heavier than in your pictures, or even saying you can ride a horse or drive stick shift when you can't (and that skill is important to the job), you have taken a coveted slot away from a talent that is right for the job and you have made the casting director look bad by not showing enough "right" options to his client. Being who you say you are is a mark of a true professional and a great way to have a long-lasting career. Alternatively, not doing this can make your career much shorter, because casting directors remember when you do these things and they will not call you back.

3 Solve their problem.

All casting directors want to do is make their client happy by delivering an amazing talent for every role they were hired to fill. All they want when you walk in that audition room is for you to be great. Really, they want you to be great. They are on your side. If you can come in prepared and confident, knowing they are your allies and not someone to fear, it can really shift your paradigm and help you operate from a more empowered space. Knowing that casting has a problem (which is needing to fill a role) and you could be the one to solve it by being the perfect person for the part can be a real game changer for you as talent.

Getting Ready for Your Audition

1 The best audition colors are bold, solid tones; stay away from black, white, or red. Dress as close to the on-camera role you are trying to win. If it's a corporate spokesperson, don't show up in your gym clothes. A great idea is to keep a suit, gym outfit, upscale outfit, and casual everyday look in your car in case you don't have time to go home before an audition.

2 Don't wear perfume. EVER! People can be really sensitive and if you give casting a migraine, it's not going to make a great impression.

3 Show up with your hair and appearance tidy, unless they have requested you to look disheveled.

4 Ladies, wear some light natural makeup (it helps how we look on camera).

5 In the audition room, ask the casting director for your mark and where they want you to look, on or off camera.

ACT 2: EXPERTS

CHAPTER 6

THE VALUE OF BEING A MEDIA EXPERT

If I've learned anything from having placed over ten thousand experts on television, both as a television producer and as CEO of TVGuestpert, it is this: *you are already an expert.* Even if you don't realize it. At the very least, you're an expert at your own life experience. Where I come in is helping people realize what their particular area of expertise is, how they can capitalize on that expertise, and how to share it beyond their existing sphere of influence.

For many people who have acquired a wealth of wisdom in their personal and professional lives, there are only so many hours in a day, days in a week, and weeks in a year that allow them to impact the greatest amount of people. This is why mass media is crucial.

I coined and trademarked the term *Guestpert* to cover the wide range of guests I was placing on television shows who were experts in their chosen fields, from the movie industry to finance, law, real estate, and relationships, to name a few. Being on TV is a significant way to share your knowledge with a larger audience that most people don't have access to otherwise through their work. It is also an effective way to promote your products, brand, company, and services.

As the head of the media development company TVGuestpert, TVGuestpert Publishing, and TVOnCameraTraining.com with offices in Silicon Beach, I oversee three hundred media leads a day from around the world. Whatever your particular area of expertise, there is a TV producer, journalist, or interviewer somewhere right now looking to book a guest with your background and credentials.

Some of the most accomplished experts in the world may be asked to teach master classes in advanced schools, or give public performance seminars at the top of their field, but that doesn't equate with readiness to be on camera. In fact, as far as the visual media is concerned it is based on short-form content; public speakers are usually skilled in long-form content. Therefore, many are surprised to learn that public speakers require the most media training to fit into the box of television news shows and talk shows in tight, precise execution of sound bites with very little in-the-moment feedback.

Everyone, even the most dynamic and extroverted personality, can use some degree of on-camera training. What is at stake is your reputation and potentially your livelihood. With citizen journalism gaining momentum and accessible in the palm of our hand through our cell phones, we can record, and be recorded, in any time and space. The ability to say what you mean, mean what you say, and not say it meanly is an important responsibility for any expert, brand, or business owner. Don't believe me? Just ask Papa John's founder, John Schnatter, or comedienne Roseanne Barr.

Remember the 87th Academy Awards red carpet coverage on E! Entertainment's Fashion Police? Veteran fashion host and darling of the show Giuliana Rancic got a case of foot-in-mouth disease with her off-the-cuff remark about Disney Channel star-turned-movie-star Zendaya's dreadlock hairstyle probably smelling like "patchouli oil ... or weed." Career-damaging comments are difficult to take back, especially if you are relying on the TV show or the host to cover your butt. This very assumption is one of the most common mistakes people make in television interviews. This is a risk business owners can't afford to make.

One of the most awkward hosting moments I can remember in my career as a television producer and media trainer was watching Steve Harvey miss-announce the Miss Universe winner. Ouch! I still cringe. Certainly, it was an excruciating moment for all who watched, and probably for Steve himself, as he announced the wrong winner.

If a blunder of this magnitude can happen to a seasoned Emmy Award–winning talk show host, where does that leave the rest of us? Especially considering that most of us have way more at stake when confronting foot-in-mouth disease than Steve Harvey. For one thing, we won't get the same amount of media opportunities to redeem ourselves in the public eye. If we are promoting and representing our message, our business, our point of view, and our reputation, the standard for our performances runs high. But if the risks of being an expert/Guestpert seem high, *the rewards are well worth it.* Those rewards can be yours with just a little greater preparation and attention.

In my previous incarnation as a television booker, I produced feminist attorney Gloria Allred as a guest for shows at CNBC and on the Geraldo daytime television show. Whether you know, like, or dislike Gloria Allred, there are a few crucial points you need to know as an aspiring media expert.

Gloria has mastered the art of being a guest expert. Netflix has a documentary, *Seeing Allred*, about Gloria Allred with Marta Kauffman as one of the producers, known previously for her role as co-creator and executive producer of the hit show *Friends*. Gloria has mastered it so well that she has the media working for her on behalf of her causes and initiatives. That should be the goal of any media expert, to have the media working for you. When I watched the Netflix documentary about someone I have had the privilege of producing, I can say definitively that she knows how to use the media. The media does not use her. She does not need to be concerned about whether or not she is liked or popular because she turns the attention to her issues, her causes, her campaigns. She has been effective at doing this for a long time. Gloria has the mastery of her own branding. She doesn't confuse her own personal self-identity with her celebrity. She uses this recognition for a purpose. If my clients could learn one thing from her, it's this: don't take media actions and interactions personally. In other words, stop counting your likes!

Princess Diana is another famous figure who flipped the media to pay attention to her causes prior to her death. One of her most famous campaigns featured Diana holding an AIDS-inflicted child in the hospital. This was unheard of at the time. She was busting the AIDS-as-leprosy stereotype with her actions. She was also recognized for standing on the ground of unexploded land mines with locals who had lost their own limbs to these very same land mines. Both Gloria and Princess Diana's use of the media is what every expert should aspire to emulate.

FX's television mini-series *The People v. O.J. Simpson* was a surprise hit, primarily because it captured so perfectly the surreal events it was based on. Attorney Johnnie Cochran masterminded a case that played out in the media and reached far beyond the courtroom because he knew the power of the narrative. No surprise, since Cochran had "made his bones" as a legal expert for years prior to that case. His was one of the most notable examples of someone knowing how to use the techniques outlined here as guest expert to sway public opinion.

Now what? Watch the shows you want to be on.

Show producers are looking for experts with a credible media platform. Their job is on the line based on the quality of the experts that they book and the guests' ability to deliver their content. And you thought the stakes were high just for you!

Producers without a publicist or PR firm are welcome to pitch a segment idea in a complete and easily digestible form. References to pitches are easily found in my first book, *Get on TV! The Insider's Guide to Pitching the Producers and Promoting Yourself* (Sourcebooks, 2006). A producer will generally want to see your headshot, bio, and chosen topic, along with (last but not least) all the talking points and beats for an entire segment. A TV segment typically runs between four and seven minutes. This pitch format will reduce the amount of work the producer has to do for the segment. Anything you can do to make the producer's job easier gets you one step closer to a confirmed booking and, most importantly, preparing you for your on-air appearance.

If and when you get called to be an expert for a talk show or a news program, make sure you respond that you are available or not available right away. When producers are hunting for their next guest expert, they put calls out in many directions. Thus the importance of a timely and enthusiastic response.

Experts often misplace the value of the host relationship as the most significant. Although it is key, the producer is the composer to any television segment, the host is the lead dancer, and you are the host's partner. The host is usually not the beginning decision maker when it comes to expert pitches. The gatekeeper is the producer.

A healthy relationship with a producer is key to your longevity on air. I worked with television producer Adam Spiegelman in the '90s on a television show for the FX network in New York City. Some twenty years later, Adam is the supervising producer for the hit shows *The Real* and VH-1's *Martha and Snoop's Potluck Dinner Party*. Adam has been TVGuestpert's guest producer at several TVOnCameraTraining.com workshops.

CHAPTER 7

INTERVIEW STYLES

Acquiring confidence and understanding about the interview format is instrumental in preparing and handling your television appearance. Let's start with the basics. There are four distinctive types of interviews you need to be aware of before you set foot in a studio or even pitch a producer. Each type has its own particular requirements in terms of your participation. Understanding the differences between interview types will give you the understanding of how the end result is assembled and your responsibility as a participant.

1. SIT-DOWN INTERVIEW. This is the most typical type of interview that you will see on *The View*, *Super Soul Sunday*, *Live with Kelly and Ryan*, and on the couch with any of your favorite morning show hosts. These are generally promotional interviews by featured actors or authors talking about their latest projects. But these types of interviews also very much include experts, or Guestperts, discussing a recent study or a current event about which they are particularly knowledgeable. What defines the sit-down interview is that it is an in-person, usually in-studio, interview with a host facilitating the discussion. These shows are live or live-to-tape, where the interview is treated as if it is live even when it is actually prerecorded; no post-production/editing will be applied to the show, except in rare instances, and almost never for the guest expert's comments, which takes me back to my earlier maxim to mean what you say and say what you mean. Wherever possible, do not say it meanly! A live-to-tape show is usually cut to time, not to content.

Release forms are required for live-to-tape shows, but not live shows. The reason for this is that it protects the show from editing to time, whereas a live show is happening in the moment, so guests can't accuse a show of manipulating their content. It is good to familiarize yourself with a guest release form prior to arriving on set, as the legal language is quite intimidating. This is why on-camera training is so important. If you are in command of your content, you won't carry the unnecessary fear that your words can and will be used against you. In the back of my first book, *Get on TV!*, I include a standard guest release form to review.

2. DEMO SEGMENT. "Demo" is short for demonstration. We recognize these segments as cooking segments, fashion segments, and beauty product or techno-gadget segments. Shows like *Rachael Ray*, Hallmark's *Home & Family*, CMT's *Pickler & Ben*, *The Today Show*, *The Doctors*, *The Dr. Oz Show*, and *Good Morning America* include typical demo-style segments where the action happens standing up at a demonstration table.

Demo segments can be in-studio or remote, as in someone's home kitchen. You want to be prepared with visual aids for these types of interviews. If it's a fashion segment, bring models. If it's a food segment, bring plates, food, and extra decorations if necessary. We are really big on making sure that our Guestperts produce a visually decorative and appealing demo segment. This is as important as the execution itself, and it's often something we like to block out during on-camera training sessions.

Demo segments are fun for hosts and particularly attractive for producers, because they easily entertain the viewers beyond the typical "talking head" segment.

If it's a tech segment, you will need to bring the items for a table display. Make everything unique and have fun with your segment. In different affiliate markets, you can repeat the same demo segment—for example, in Nashville and San Diego—since you aren't repeating the same audience.

We had an experience recently sending out an expert to do a demo segment that I hope will serve as a cautionary tale. Since we are in the Los Angeles TV market, which is the second-largest television market in the nation, we often send our less experienced clients to smaller markets, where the risk is less. It gives them good exposure and brings something unique to a local audience. In this cautionary tale, the demo segment pitched was titled "Weeds in Your Backyard that Make a Great Salad." As we pitched it to the producer, the idea was that the guest would show the weeds in a big display demo fashion—a variety of plants in pots varying in size and decorated around the guest and the host—and include a bowl of what the weeds would look like after the salad was prepared, as in a cooking segment.

Unfortunately, the client didn't return our preproduction calls to discuss the demo, nor did she rehearse and block out the segment. We all know this spells trouble right away. We received, instead, an email that she had spoken to the producer the night before for her pre-interview, and the producer informed her that bringing a salad was not necessary. This was because the client had no props prepared other than a few bushels of weeds. When we watched the show live, the demo segment had been reduced to a sit-down interview, or the "talking head" segment. This meant my client had missed a great opportunity for a really cool demo segment that we could have used to place her on other like-minded television shows on the Food Network, where the format is based on only demo segments or cooking at the counter. Such are the perils of being unprepared for a demo segment and the unknown loss of future opportunities of positive exposure.

3. SATELLITE INTERVIEW. This is the type of "box" interview you see on breaking news stories on CNN, HLN, and FOX News Channel where they talk via satellite to an expert who is on location outside of the home studio. In my media coaching opinion, satellite interviews require the most skill, experience, and mastery. In the earlier days of my producing career, the guest on a satellite interview would watch the feedback monitor in real time through the actual camera that he was looking into.

Unfortunately, this feature proved to be cost prohibitive, so guests no longer receive real-time feedback of personal facial expressions or nonverbal cues from the on-set hosts or from the other guests in other locations. This means that all the feedback is coming to the guest expert only through audio via an earpiece.

During a satellite interview, you are often in an empty room by yourself with a television monitor, staring directly into a camera with a feedback line in your ear.

Here are a couple of tips to ensure a successful satellite guest appearance.

- Don't look away from the camera. You will no longer give the appearance of a trustworthy, knowledgeable expert on the subject at hand. It is also distracting, as viewers will try and imagine what you're looking at off camera that's more compelling than looking at them!
- Be mindful of all your facial expressions while maintaining a relaxed posture. The camera is always aimed at your face. It's fine to be relaxed, but make sure you project the attitude of an authoritative expert. Remember, even when you are not speaking, you may be on a split screen with the host or another satellite guest, so it's important to project this attitude and confidence at all times.
- Don't assume you know when you are on or off camera. Don't say or do anything out of place that you don't want caught on camera until you are safely out of the camera's range and unmic'd. I coach my clients to assume the camera is always rolling and taping even if they're not on the screen. You never know how quickly your camera will be turned on, and you do

not want to be caught in an awkward or uncomfortable position.

- More of these interviews are being conducted via Skype these days because it is cost effective. The quality of a Skype interview is never as clean visually as a satellite interview, but Skype is much cheaper and can be more immediate.
- Being on TV in a Skype interview is never an excuse for a guest expert to allow for poor quality, uneven picture, and/or bad lighting. Trained Guestperts will know how to level their Skype shot with the framing of the host on the set. Trained Guestperts will know how to look into the eye of the computer camera instead of at their computer screen. Again, you must avoid the natural instincts to watch the host and yourself on screen. This is something that can and should be practiced, especially if you are someone who covers breaking news and want to be a go-to guest who's always on call.
- Skype with a friend and have her take screenshots so you can see how your setup looks, to ensure that you have the best setup possible for your interview.

With TVGuestpert, there are opportunities that come up for hosting or recurring Guestpert appearances. We always want to make sure our clients' skills in this arena are sharp and professional.

Phillip Andrew Barbb, Emmy-nominated TV producer, media coach, and speaker, has conducted well over five hundred Skype auditions in his career and is a big believer that prep makes perfect. As Barbb says, "Whenever anyone comes on Skype for audition, the more prepared they are with the technology of Skype, the more professional the audition feels."

According to him, even simple things like good lighting and solid audio can make the difference between a successful audition and a disastrous one. Despite TVGuestpert's best prepping intentions, one of our Guestperts went on live television while Skyping from his bathroom. It was his best attempt to find a quiet place, but you could still see the towel rack behind his head. It was so distracting and uncomfortable for me, I could barely watch the segment.

"I know at TVGuestpert, you rehearse the Skype technology with your clients before you allow them to audition. All of this counts in the overall decision of whether or not I will want to work professionally with this person on camera or on the show I am about to produce," says Barbb.

"Sometimes, I eat up as much as twenty minutes helping a potential talent just to get their Skype ready. It's not fun, and it makes my job more complicated. What most people don't know is that when they are doing a Skype audition with me, thirty other people will see it. I cannot show my casting team and the executive department a sloppy Skype. I just won't. So I will do my best to support the talent in giving them the best possible chance, but even with this said, it's to their own disadvantage when the technology interferes and precedes their performance.

"Pay attention to what is happening in your background. Fix your blinds. I don't want to see your dog run behind you. Secure your space. Nothing should distract from the talent's ability to perform. It's essentially an employment opportunity. Would this go on in a job interview?

"It's important to remember how your segments will be viewed by the people who have the power to hire you again or not. They're thinking to themselves: Does the potential talent understand how this whole process works or not? Do they demonstrate a desire to learn? Showing a desire to understand this stuff will translate to the things that will benefit them the most.

"Remember, whether it airs or not, other people are going to see your Skype audition. It may even be seen by someone's cousin who is not supposed to share it with anyone else. You know how this goes. Every second you are on screen, you are accountable for how you are communicating verbally and nonverbally."

You read it right there from Phillip Andrew Barbb! That is why Shannon and I are happy you are reading this book right now. In this day and age, if it is digitally recorded, it can and may be used against you, and we want it to be used FOR YOU!

4. ENG, OR FIELD INTERVIEW. The fourth style of interview is the ENG (Electronic News Gathering), also known as a field interview. *20/20* is a good example and can appear to be a sit-down interview to the viewer. What defines this interview is that it usually takes place outside a studio and airs in a time frame after being recorded. These interviews are taped or filmed, depending on location, by a crew that brings their equipment, which typically includes cameras, lights, and audio, to that location. This could happen in your living room. Usually, the show will interweave other footage and interviews into one segment to air.

Even if your interview happens to take place in a studio, the show will be adding features such as B-roll, or host narrative, through post-production. In the end, what you say in your primary interview will be chosen after you have been taped. This leaves you, the guest expert, with very little control over the final segment.

Make sure this last bit sticks in your head. Everything that comes out of your mouth on camera matters, as you won't have an opportunity to take it back. I fundamentally believe this to be true about all the interview styles. You simply cannot expect the third party (the show or producers) to cover or protect you from what you do or do not say.

Understanding these four basic types of interviews for broadcast and traditional television allows you to understand as well as how the final product will be recorded, assembled, and distributed. This knowledge will make you a better-educated and empowered interviewee, and more effective in delivering your content.

According to life coach and frequent Guestpert Lisa Haisha, "Having done dozens of in-studio sit-down interviews, I cruised through the brutal five minutes in the hot seat with *20/20*'s field interview simply by being so well prepared for this style of interview."

Lisa's sit-down interview was an ENG/field-style taping. This technique of interviewing for electronic news gathering or field pieces is also how reality-style television shows are produced.

My genre of television producing credits falls under the category of "non-scripted," according to the Producers Guild of America and the Writers Guild of America. A scripted producer works, writes, and creates for fiction shows such as *The Big Bang Theory*, *Grey's Anatomy*, *Stranger Things*, *Game of Thrones*, and the like.

Despite my breed of producers being called "non-scripted," trust me—we always write a script. These categories are actually based on salary rates, not actual work style. Therefore, it is misleading to believe that reality shows are not written out. At the very least, reality shows are laid out in writing and hit very specific story arcs and talking points.

In reality shows, which feature a form of ENG or field-style interviews or tapings, the segment or show gets edited for content and sound bites, whereas live-to-tape or live sit-down interviews do not rely on editing or post-production. Often during tapings for ENGs and field pieces, the producer or the host, who is not on camera with you, will ask you to repeat his questions as part of the top of your answer in the most natural way possible. You have to remember, you are being interviewed, but his presence and questions will be edited out of the final product of the show.

For example:

—Producer to Expert: "Jacquie, what has been the most rewarding experience of running your own business?"

—It is instinctual to respond in the following manner: "Guiding people toward success by using the media opportunities for growing their core business."

—Instead, the expert prepared for this type of interview will respond, "The most rewarding experience of running my own business is guiding people toward success by using the media opportunities for growing their core business."

According to Phillip Andrew Barbb, "*The talk-back questioning* is a really sophisticated interview technique. And as a producer and editor myself, I am often editing the show in my head as the expert is speaking. So I know how I can move things around or where my edit points are by what they are saying. I try not to interrupt the flow of conversation with this specific direction if they do not know it already or do not remember the prompt prior to their flow. As a producer there is a fine balance in keeping the interview natural without having the expert overproduced."

Barbb continues to say, "If you are talking about specifics, people should always use proper names. For example, 'I love him' doesn't work on camera. 'I love Michael, my fiancé' is specific and usable."

With reality shows, there is no on- or off-camera interviewer. The producer gives the cast hit points, and the dialogue is generally free flowing. Editing is left exclusively to the discretion of the show during post-production.

Understanding the various interview styles holds the guests accountable for their own content and messaging, and enables them to understand how the show will shape their content. They are now in a position to completely manage and command what they say, state, or answer without becoming a victim to the perception that the experience is beyond their control. As producers, we know that it's only the "green" guests who blame the show or the show's producers when they're not happy with the outcome of their appearance. Don't be a victim to your own lack of knowledge!

You are now empowered to be the master of your own delivery no matter what the format; this in turn will make it easier to view each potential interview as an opportunity to achieve your overall media goals.

We're offering (and strongly encouraging) a paradigm shift, so that you can have a better, more positive approach to each interview you participate in. You're not a victim anymore, and producers aren't out to sabotage you. They're on your side. They want you to succeed. If you look good, they look good. The investment is the same.

Nevertheless, if they have to teach the process to every guest expert booked on their show, that will create unwanted producorial drag. Guess what? A more seasoned, better prepared guest expert suddenly looks to be a heck of a lot easier and a way better bet. This is why you so often see the same faces in the media. The producer and the show can count on these experts to deliver. We are advocating that you cut in front of the line with your full knowledge of the process, and introduce some fresh faces (i.e., YOURS) into that tried-and-true rotation!

Remember, what producers are interested in first and foremost is good content and good content delivery. Experts are interchangeable. If the producer is looking for a guest with a certain expertise or opinion, she will seek out the best on-camera expert to provide her with the goods. This means a camera-ready expert has a significant advantage over all others.

In other words, a producer will take a less qualified expert to deliver the exact same content if that expert is better on camera than a more qualified expert who is less experienced and less commanding on air.

Empower your performance!

CHAPTER 8

ANATOMY OF A SEGMENT

On-camera training has more to do with being in command of your content than your physical hand gestures. Knowing the boundaries of your content begins with breaking it down and performing what we call the anatomy of a segment for your overall hot topic.

Hot topics are overall show segment pitches, written and created by the experts to create opportunities to get themselves booked. In other words, they're producer bait! A producer in turn can use these topics to get inspiration for future show segments. A hot topic can include news hooks for timely appeal, but only when appropriate. Keep in mind that producers are not booking you for you, your book, or your product. They want you for the expertise and insight you offer on the topic at hand. The content of the show segment is really the star; you're there because you are the appropriate and best expert on camera to make the star look good, i.e., to provide fresh angles that help the audience stay compelled by this segment.

The format of a pitch for television is different from a sales pitch you might present to a customer, client, reading audience, or lecture audience. Producers prefer to receive pitches when they are done in a way that follows certain guidelines. There is a real art and a science to creating effective pitches. The format of a pitch is important. That's why we've created a form for you that lays out this format, and it's one that will allow producers to be able to visualize what your show segment is going to look like.

The moral of the story is that hot topics become the precursor for your speaking points.

There are seven parts to the anatomy of a segment:

1 **NEWS HOOKS:** This is the hot-topic umbrella or the topic title of your pitch.

2 **YOUR OPENING SOUND BITE:** The first sentence out of your mouth needs to reestablish and further your credibility to the viewers as to why they should stay on this channel and continue watching you.

3 **SPEAKING POINTS:** Your list of speaking points.

4 THE TAKE-HOME INFORMATION: The information that you impart for the viewers; the what that they are learning by investing their precious time in watching your appearance.

5 ANCHOR STORY: The one personal story that makes you unique and usually ties specifically with why you became an expert in the field that you are in. This becomes part of your Deck of Cards.

6 DECK OF CARDS: Your baseline content, stories that define your expertise.

7 YOUR PLUG: The payoff for your appearance, such as your book, website, event, podcast, or feature film.

1. News Hooks.

The hook is the title of the show segment. We recommend making this clever or compelling. For example, if you are pitching a topic about how people can lose weight by exercising with their dog, you could title it "How Your Dog Can Help You Lose Weight." Big snoozer, right? Instead, we'd strongly suggest a title more along the lines of "Fighting Fat with Furry Friends." See the difference? Sometimes all it takes is a simple play on words to create an engaging hook.

On the day that President Trump's Hollywood Walk of Fame star was destroyed with a pick axe, the editors at *Huffington Post* crafted this bit of cleverness by titling an article "Trump Star Struck." No matter which end of the political spectrum you lean toward, that is a catchy hook.

If you were pitching a segment idea about whether or not the local city government should approve a beekeeping project, rather than calling it "Why the City Needs a Beekeeping Facility" you might call it "To Bee or Not to Bee in the City." Sometimes it's the simple shock factor that works.

Watch the shows you want to be on. How do they tease segments when they go to a commercial break? An example with our topic earlier would be "When we come back, we'll talk about *Fighting Fat with Furry Friends*." How long are their guest experts on air? Are most of their segments how-to? Do they use their guest experts to chime in on personal story segments? Do they have demo segments? The answers to these questions will help you craft the most engaging hook for that show.

I am a big believer that content is key to any successful booking and subsequent appearance. I can say that paying attention to news hooks is as important in the pitching process as is the execution itself.

In *Get on TV!*, I discuss news hooks as relevant to creating pitches such as:

Current Events
Holidays / Anniversaries
New Study / Statistics
Celebrities

2. Opening Sound Bite.

The most important words of your television segment are the first words that come out of your mouth. I call this prime real estate. After all, as one of my favorite clichés goes, you never get a second chance to make a first impression. This impression establishes your relevance and value to the topic being addressed.

Often, the host's lead-in question ("How are you?") or lead-in introduction ("Welcome to the show.") is often not the best setup or lead-in for brand messaging. It's wasted airtime for you and your segment. Filler words. A loss of real estate value to the expert's overall goals.

The bold guest expert will recognize this and say, "I'm good, Doug, but really concerned about the opioid crisis that's killing our country right now. I've seen firsthand the wreckage of our policies as an addiction specialist."

Another opening can be "As a doctor who's treated hundreds of patients suffering from bipolar disorder ..." or "Because of my experience working on the front lines of the eco sustainability movement in the fashion industry ..."

Instead, many guests answer with, "Thanks for having me on the show." Then they pause and wait for the host to lay out their first real question. Thirty seconds burn up. Viewers have changed the channel. These guests have missed an opportunity to come out with a bang to the audience by contextualizing their expertise and stating a position on the topic at hand.

In response to the host intro, you want to add additional credits that are relevant to the specific topic, reestablish the topic and include why you are qualified to speak on it, then begin your point of view without wasting time. This also assists the viewers at home as to why they want to stay further engaged in the segment as opposed to changing the channel. Get right to it!

For example, a host might say, "To tell us why digital media is here to stay is Jacquie Jordan, a two-time Emmy-nominated television producer and a *New York Times* bestselling publisher. Welcome, Jacquie."

My opening sound bite in response to this introduction would be the following: "Thank you, Jim. Ten years ago, when I wrote my first book, *Get on TV! The Insider's Guide to Pitching the Producers and Promoting Yourself*, I already knew that television was undergoing a radical change, which started with the DVR and the disruption of commercial advertising as we knew it. Those of us in the business were faced with a clear choice: adapt or slowly become extinct. I chose life, Jim!"

An untrained expert can burn up to thirty seconds of airtime in pleasantries before getting into the segment. On radio, guests often forget that the listener has been listening continuously, and that the guest is the only one who just entered the room. For me, as an advocate for my experts' businesses, pleasantries are problematic, as they offer little to no value. No permissions needed here. Forget everything you think about your appearance being an interview. The word "interview" is an erroneous description of your time on camera. It is a well-orchestrated tango. The producer is the choreographer, the host is the dance lead, and the guest is the dance follower. It is structured, but allows for organic flow to the timing of the moment.

A contextualized opening sound bite will immediately launch you, the host, and the audience into the heart of your content and get your segment off to a roaring start by reestablishing why viewers should commit the next few minutes of their life to you. This opening sound bite is also a meaningful way to define your expertise, while simultaneously tying it into your branding and delivering the prescribed segment at hand. This is an essential tool to use without becoming a pitch person, which is a big no-no to audiences and, especially, producers!

Longtime guest expert Dr. Carole Lieberman executed a very effective opening sound bite on a FOX affiliate recently after the host used over thirty seconds to introduce both Carole and her book, *Bad Girls*. That is a lot of TV real estate for the host to eat up for a segment only slotted for six minutes, which is why understanding your content is important for your on-camera appearance. The first words out of Dr. Lieberman's mouth cut right to the chase: "When I wrote *Bad Boys* all the guys were asking, 'When are you going to write *Bad Girls*?' Well, here it is."

Dr. Carole Lieberman, seasoned TV expert of over twenty years, needed only one sentence to let viewers know who she was, an author with more books to her credit than the one she'd be promoting on the show, and why she was there: to offer the flip side of a gender story. That is the art of an opening sound bite. By taking advantage of the opening sound bite as an opportunity to communicate a brand statement on a relevant hot topic, the expert paves the way for the rest of the segment. It will now be that much easier for the expert to speak with intentional purpose, and for the audience to understand why the expert is participating on the show.

If you watch TV closely, most experts simply answer the questions the host asks. They're way too literal. Politicians, of course, do the exact opposite, taking the art of dodging a question to the other annoying extreme. At TVGuestpert, we are serving two interests: our B2B and our B2C. We are providing our producing community with camera-ready experts who know how to deliver their content in a right-on-time, agreed-upon manner. This is our business to business (aka "B2B"). We are also servicing our clients by supporting their goals or businesses by booking their appearances. This is our business to consumer ("B2C"). In serving both masters, we are there to make sure the choreography of this pre-orchestrated tango comes off flawlessly while delivering entertainment and delight to all participants ... especially the viewers at home!

3. Speaking Points.

Think in terms of small, digestible, and TV-friendly sound bites. They should be things that you might actually say that make a point. They should be short and concise.

Speaking points usually accompany a pitch under a hot-topic title following the opening sound bite. They are the answers that you provide to the producer and host in anticipation of questions the host may ask you on air. They become agreed-upon content. This agreed-upon content becomes the composition for the choreography of your segment. The practice of consistently writing out these speaking points helps our clients develop their opinions and/or expertise on a particular topic at a particular time period. It also allows TVGuestpert, representing our B2B and B2C, to lay out the score for the upcoming choreographed tango, which will become a dance and a segment.

The practice of writing up speaking points thus has several benefits:

1. It will help you acquire the booking opportunity.
2. It establishes your unique point of view, distinguishing you from other experts of similar experience competing for the same booking opportunity.
3. It puts you in control of representing your brand messaging.
4. It serves as an informal agreement between you and the producer who will be representing you to the show and the show's hierarchy of decision makers, including the host.
5. It sets the expectation for what you will be delivering on air.

A red flag of a green guest is when the guest expert expects TVGuestpert to pitch the host of the show rather than the producer of the show. Such a guest doesn't understand the power, influence, and responsibility the producer has in laying out, designing, and creating the narrative for the host on the show or the segment.

I often suggest participants think of their speaking points as sound bites you would share with a stranger at a cocktail party. Simple, tight content that contextualizes who you are, your experience, and your point of view on a topic. It shouldn't be a lengthy dissertation. If it's long on paper, then it will be too long out of your mouth.

Producers pre-write their scripts, even for supposedly "unscripted" news or reality shows. That's because they already know the point of view they are looking to have represented; they are simply plugging in an expert to deliver that message.

At TVGuestpert, when we present speaking points to producers, we're trying to help them flesh out their vision, or to up-level what they may have preconceived by offering a point of view they hadn't thought of themselves. After all, the producer isn't the expert, YOU ARE!

You might be asked to submit your speaking points to a producer in advance or to discuss them during the pre-interview. Your speaking points serve as the unspoken and unwritten contract between you and the producer of the show. Regardless of which speaking points you actually cover in the segment, which might come down to the flow of the conversation or what questions the host chooses in the moment to ask you, the speaking points are understood by all to represent the spirit of what you intend to talk about and the spirit of what you are there to deliver.

You had better be prepared to handle a host who offers up questions that might stray slightly from your point of view and the agreed-upon content. When that happens, it's your job to acknowledge the question, then redirect the focus and the conversation back to your speaking points. An example would be, "That's a great question, Jim, and it reminds me of the importance of medication ..."

By that same token, even though a producer might not be micromanaging what a host asks you or what answers you provide to certain questions, she knows from your speaking points what to expect from your messaging.

During the pre-interview process between the Guestpert and the producer, the producer will ask the Guestpert to modify how she tells a particular speaking point, if the content needs to be redirected. This same producer should also review the speaking points in the green room before you are walked on set by the stage or floor manager, and before you are seated with a microphone on in the interview chair.

Sound bites can contain such elements as follows:

1 Personal stories
2 Referencing your findings in your book
3 Points of debate
4 Contextualizing your expertise in relation to the topic
5 Statistics or other substantiating content

When I appeared on the cable show *America Trends*, I was booked to discuss Sinclair Broadcasting's *Scripted News: Fake News* controversial statement that they had literally hundreds of anchors read across the country. Below are my written speaking points of how I intertwined trending news hooks like Laura Ingraham and FOX News losing advertisers to reinforce my point of view on the topic point:

OPENING SOUND BITE: As a professional media trainer, I help my clients script out their content. Creating content is a big part of how TV is done.

SPEAKING POINT #1: The way news is done is that it's pulled from AP and Reuters, and syndicated shows are also pulled from their national network (i.e., Sinclair Media). Corporations do own lots of affiliates. Lots of corporations have smaller affiliate companies and consistent messaging that gets passed around that is expected to be adhered to throughout the company by its employees. So with all that being said, it really isn't that unheard of for similar scripted stories to be passed around within a news organization like this.

SPEAKING POINT #2: It's a large country, where the culture and climate of certain areas really range. It's not uncommon to make an effort to streamline and make consistent messaging throughout areas that might otherwise be subject to regionalisms.

SPEAKING POINT #3: When I work with my clients, we work hard to craft messaging that is consistent with their brand and professional practices. Crafting stories and content is a BIG part of how news is done.

SPEAKING POINT #4: This is not a new practice in the media. What is new is that viewers are having a significant impact on outlets and the backlash from these types of incidents like companies pulling their advertising because of viewers boycotting stations, networks, and programs.

SPEAKING POINT #5 (news hook reference): For example, Laura Ingraham just lost Ace Hardware as an advertiser, and she has had to take a vacation. This boycott was from a social media post. Social media is creating a platform with journalists who before were expected to be neutral at their job. Now they are given a stage to speak their mind and voice their opinions like never before. And the backlash from doing this can be seen almost in real time.

SPEAKING POINT #6: It's kind of like the Wild West in media and social media.

SPEAKING POINT #7: As a media coach, it is important to know your brand and messaging and keep your talking points consistent with those things. Because this is how news is done.

SPEAKING POINT #8: The climate today, and our society really, is on high alert to what is being disseminated by the media. It's a sensitive and polarizing time with the swirling of fake news v. real news. It will be incredibly interesting to see how this all plays out and how it might ultimately change media and how we consume our news and information. I do think there is an opportunity to pause and realize that this might just be a corporation doing what corporations do. And not to say that what has happened is right, but it may be more thoughtless as standard operating procedure than being an evil empire spreading information to brainwash viewers. Just food for thought!

Business Insider reached out to Mark Cuban to ask about his top tips for potential lottery winners. Cuban shared this expert advice with his local *Dallas Morning News*, and in doing so, showed that this shark knows killer speaking points.

Hot Topic: Top Tips for Potential Lottery Winners

- *The first thing you should do is hire a tax attorney.*
- *Don't take the lump sum. You don't want to blow it all in one spot.*
- *If you weren't happy yesterday, you won't be happy tomorrow. It's money. It's not happiness.*

- *If you were happy yesterday, you are going to be a lot happier tomorrow. It's money. Life gets easier when you don't have to worry about the bills.*
- *Tell all your friends and relatives no. They will ask. Tell them no. If you are close to them, you already know who needs help and what they need. Feel free to help SOME, but talk to your accountant before you do anything and remember this: no one needs $1 million for anything. Anyone who asks is not your friend.*
- *You don't become a smart investor when you win the lottery. Don't make investments. You can put it in the bank and live comfortably. Forever. You will sleep a lot better knowing you won't lose money.*

Wow, Cuban packs a whole lot of wisdom and life lessons into these short, sweet speaking points! My advice to aspiring experts is to try and use this template when you're first mapping out your speaking points. What Cuban has done here, and what I'd love for you all to be able to do, is to boil down the essence of what you want to say into short, digestible, meaningful bite-sized pieces. Once you've done that, you can expand outward from there, confident in the knowledge you're building atop a solid sustainable foundation. Regardless of what you think of him, Cuban is a pro all aspiring experts can all learn from.

4. The Take-Home Information.

Take-home information is probably one of the more important styles of speaking points, as it represents the value that the viewer will receive from your content.

When I was promoting my book *Get on TV! The Insider's Guide to Pitching the Producer and Promoting Yourself*, I did an appearance on my book tour that covered how to lose weight eating chocolate. I know, not a topic that seems even remotely connected to getting on TV.

What happened was I used the "Losing Weight Eating Chocolate" as my "hook." Allow me to expand. First, I established my credibility in my opening sound bite as to why I was a qualified expert: "I'm a behind-the-scenes producer and media consultant. While writing my book *Get on TV!*, I saw the photo of myself on the cover and wondered, *Am I the image that I want to portray?* I may never have struggled with a weight issue; I was, however, aware that I was an M&M popper."

The take-home information in my speaking points became about how the average American consumes eleven pounds of chocolate a year, and at the rate I was going, I was not headed in a healthy direction.

As I qualified myself along the way, I included some interesting facts about the health benefits of chocolate that many people did not know. Raw chocolate has no processed sugar, for those of us who are addicted to sugar. Because raw chocolate isn't cooked, nor processed, it still has the magnesium that most women inherently crave. Raw cacao was used as money currency during the Mayan days.

But that currency would expire, as raw chocolate only lasts in storage for about five years. Chocolate comes from the seed of a beautiful fruit pod off trees, so once upon a time, money grew on trees!

I didn't need to be a registered dietician to be an expert in this particular story that I used to plug my book. I created the need to tell the story, which in turn landed me on the cover of *Woman's World magazine.*

5. Anchor Story.

Your anchor story is an important part of your pitch to a producer, as it signals what makes you unique as an individual. It's your personal hook that separates you from the pack, so to speak. Maybe you had a near-death experience that set you on the path to becoming a healer and writing a book. An anchor story could also be about the allergies you had to overcome that led you to creating an environmentally friendly cosmetics product line. Or how you spiced up your sex life in your marriage AND found love after fifty, and now you want to help other couples do the same. One of the reasons an anchor story is so vital in helping you get booked is that it's what makes you memorable to a producer. It's the story that defines the why. The why you do what you do. The most frequently booked experts all have one.

During your actual on-air segment, your anchor story can serve any number of functions. It could impact the way the host introduces you, and the lead of your story, and/or the central topic you're there to talk about. It could define the anatomy of the entire segment. It may also be something that won't lead the segment but will emerge out of your storytelling.

As important as an anchor story is in the pitch to the producer, be aware that at times it might not be relevant to the topic at hand and may never be brought up at all. For example, if a producer is looking to book an attorney to speak on a case as a legal expert, she'll need to know what makes the attorney stand out as an on-air personality, or what makes him or his expertise unique. Chances are his anchor story isn't likely to be an important element of the eventual segment. In this example, the attorney is being interviewed as a legal expert brought in to speak about a celebrity trial, a new bill, or a new law going into effect. It's pretty much set in stone that he's not going to give the host anything personal. This doesn't necessarily mean he's going to be boring or dry. It just means that his responsibilities as a guest will most likely lean toward providing simple answers to the host's questions.

6. Deck of Cards: Your Baseline Content.

One of the essential baseline tools that I believe all experts should include in their own professional content tool kit is what I call the deck of cards. It can be used as often as the expert needs, or when required as she shuffles through her speaking points for any on-camera appearance.

Your deck of cards is your twelve speaking points that define who you are, why you do what you do, and what the world needs to know about you that makes you unique. When properly formulated, a deck of cards will become a handy tool in your media appearances that will help contextualize for the audience who you are and what it is you do.

Circulating on YouTube is a compilation video of Lady Gaga resequencing the speaking points as part of her deck of cards as to how she came to play the role opposite Bradley Cooper in *A Star is Born*. It's a classic example of having a deck of standard generic content points available.

My being punk'd in Sacha Baron Cohen's movie *Bruno* is one of my twelve speaking points in my deck of cards. I'll share that story with you in a moment. If I entertain you with that story as part of my deck of cards (which is quite entertaining, if I do say so myself), it clearly lets you know the following: a) who I am; b) my standard of professional excellence; and c) what it is I do for a living. This crazy anecdote allows me to give a contextualized experience about what it is I do, without the hard-core elevator pitch of "I am Jacquie. I am a CEO and two-time Emmy-nominated television producer who operates a media development and publishing company out of Silicon Beach, California." Sure, that statement delivers the information, but not in as entertaining a fashion. This piece of information is always better when quickly delivered in an opening sound bite.

For the purposes of a deck of cards, these speaking points must be so unique to you that no other expert could use them. A deck of cards can consist of the anecdotal stories that define your expertise. If I were being interviewed about my company or my job, one of the stories from my deck of cards would include a shortened version of the following memorable anecdote that occurred one December morning a few years ago.

Our company, Jacquie Jordan Inc./TVGuestpert.com, had been booked to do a media consultation for a German TV personality who wanted to do a celebrity fashion show. We were told we'd be observing a focus group screening the pilot. I was asked if I would mind if they taped the consultation. I didn't have a problem with that, as I've had several of our company's services recorded.

When I arrived at the focus group in Sherman Oaks, I was quickly sequestered in a green room. I carefully read the release form (as all experts should!), and saw that it waived all my rights to any claims for future financial remuneration beyond what our company was being paid for our services. There was so much language about not making monetary claims that I thought, "Wow! They're really optimistic about the potential of this pilot selling and becoming a hit." I was impressed with their bravado and confidence.

When I was given the go-ahead to enter the control booth that overlooks the focus group, I misstepped my cue and walked in on a man hugging a woman.

No harm, no foul. They simply asked me to exit and reenter. When I did, I was introduced to an over-the-top character named Bruno … who promptly offered me champagne at 10 a.m.! I immediately noticed that the focus group was completely miscast for what I thought was a celebrity fashion TV pilot. Instead, it was a crowd of fifty-plus gray-haired, Midwestern-type men who could not have been easy to round up in Los Angeles.

In fulfilling what I thought was my job for the day, I began asking questions about the expectations for the show and the goals of its producers. Bruno started talking about all the Hollywood celebrity guests he wanted to have on the show. I told him he needed to be careful.

"It's so hard to get A-list celebrities to appear on a show like this," I warned him. "If you don't cautiously navigate the appropriate channels (agents, publicists, lawyers, etc.), you'll turn into Sacha Baron Cohen's famous character Borat, chasing Pamela Anderson across the country for an interview."

I had unwittingly made the reference while looking Sacha Baron Cohen square in the eye. Not only had I just made a reference to Sacha Baron Cohen's first film Borat, but ten minutes into what I thought was a normal job, I realized that I was now in his next film, Bruno.

What's a professional television producer/media consultant to do? It was like time had stopped. I looked around and thought, *Please don't tell me they constructed this whole scene* (and of course the producer in me is quickly adding up the budget for this moment) around the potential of my reactions to his character's antics?

Should I stay or should I go? That was the million-dollar question. However, in that moment, I didn't think it was my million dollars that was at stake. So, here I was, waking up in a movie and wondering, *Do I bust it? or Do I keep going?* Being the consummate professional that I am, I stayed for the entire two-hour filming of my punk'd appearance in the *Bruno* experience.

In the Alice in Wonderland way in which I was punk'd, I also ended up randomly at the very first test screening of Bruno, in a packed audience of eighteen thirty-five-year-old men wearing baseball caps. I sat nervously, wondering what the final product would be. I didn't make the cut. I don't think my reactions were shocking enough. But the scene I was supposed to be in was in the movie.

For better or worse, I was replaced by two over-fifty-year-old heterosexual men, who figuratively and literally drank the champagne. The shorter version still makes for a natural speaking point for my deck of cards, as it's an engaging story. For example, "I know all my clients are capable and trained for any media interview. If I can be punk'd by Sacha Baron Cohen and good enough in my job not to make his final cut, which was a prank, then my clients are capable of the same professionalism and ability to handle their content on air."

7. Your Plug.

This unspoken trade-out refers to the value of your television appearance as real estate. The exchange for your time and talent is your "plug," aka the "For Sale" sign you get to hang on the lawn. A plug can be your book, your website, your business, or your event.

Plugging is what celebrities do every time they are on a late-night show. They entertain you with one or two personal stories, but they always plug the upcoming film they're starring in.

Most shows, networks, and stations will give you a direct or an indirect plug. A direct plug is when the host mentions your book by title and shows a picture of it, or, better yet, holds the book up in her hands toward the camera.

An indirect plug is when the show, network, or station directs the viewer to the show's website for your information. Usually on their site, they will include more information about you as the expert, with the topic written out and a possible hyperlink to your web page.

Appearances featuring indirect plugs usually do not pay. They are considered promotional appearances, because you are receiving your plug in exchange for your expertise and time. This is a win for the show and a win for you. This nonfinancial arrangement allows the network, show, or station to not pay for your content. In news this is particularly important, as it allows the program to be neutral of buying a point of view.

The problem in advocating our clients or Guestperts in these situations is when the client doesn't have a well-defined plug, i.e., a clear call to action, or a pressing need for the viewer to respond. This can be an event or the release of a book.

When we advocate for business owners or experts who are in the process of building their media platform, having a good plug and the infrastructure to properly process the call to action is important. This is the value of translating the appearance to the business or client's goals.

We once tuned in to a guest on a popular SiriusXM radio show, then listened in horror as the host poked fun at the fact that the guest had no online or social media presence. That left the host with literally no place specific to direct his listeners for more information to find out about this fabulous guest. This also means that our paying client missed out on the opportunity at hand to translate the publicity value to his own platform. Other guests booked on the show have received business calls and instantly had more followers, business, and follow-ups to their appearance.

This is why we call ourselves a media development company and not just a public relations firm; we are interested in helping our clients cultivate and develop their platforms through the judicious use of plugs.

WORKSHEET

INTRODUCTION: (written for host to say, but introducing YOU, the guest)

STATE HOT TOPIC FACT/ NEWS HOOK: (as the host would introduce the topic)

HOST INTRO GUEST NAME: Joining us now is …

HOST STATES GUEST'S CREDIT #1:

HOST STATES GUEST'S CREDIT #2:

HOST SETS UP GUEST'S POINT OF VIEW: Either statement or question

Written speaking points that Guest would say

GUEST RESPONSES:

OPENING SOUND BITE:

In my experience as …

What I can tell you …

<insert name of person you are speaking with, if he or she is on camera too>

SPEAKING POINT: <requalify experience > <new content point with fact>

SPEAKING POINT: <requalify experience > <new content point with fact>

TAKE-HOME INFORMATION: <what is the viewer/listener going to learn or take away>

TAKE-HOME INFORMATION: <what is the viewer/listener going to learn or take away>

TAKE-HOME INFORMATION: <what is the viewer/listener going to learn or take away>

WRAP-UP: <Include Plug>

CHAPTER 9

EXPERTS IN DEMAND

Understanding mass-media content narrative waves is important for creating your on-air opportunities. My analogy is that your content is a surfboard catching waves of news cycles; therefore, it's important to know the arc of breaking news stories because, depending on your area of expertise, as a bookable expert you want to understand where you will fall in the requested timeline of appearances. When a tragedy strikes, for instance, the first layer of bookings will go to public officials, eyewitnesses, people on the scene. The media is looking for the government body to identify, declare, and detail what has officially occurred. The media is also looking for eyewitnesses and people on the scene to share with viewers the details from their perspective as to what has happened. Government officials, public spokespersons, and eyewitnesses get the first round of screen time. Government or law enforcement officials drop the official statements, whereas eyewitnesses color the details to the incident. These experts are rotated in the first twenty-four hours of a breaking news cycle. Many of these interviews end up being satellite-style or ENG-style interviews because of the last-minute nature of these bookings.

On Day 2 of a breaking news story, the digesters are called in for an appearance. Digesters don't necessarily need to have any direct connection to the actual event; they are used to help viewers process—or digest—the experience and, when necessary, help us understand how to prevent something similar from happening again. This can be a former government or public official or someone with a personal story that relates to the experience that either the victims or the eyewitnesses have gone through. Day 2 is also when the booking requests will come for therapists, psychologists, life coaches, psychiatrists, and grief and trauma experts. Producers and bookers often start from an M.D. or Ph.D. and/or a credible institution, then work their way backwards in credentials. Often, you'll see these experts in studio at the desk for a live interview.

On Day 3, even if new information is being revealed, producers begin to push for "polarity." In other words, they are now looking for the two sides of the argument, or more if possible—the victim-and-the-victimizer conversation. This is where it becomes critical that an expert be willing to take a side. Weaker, more gray or neutral opinions get pushed farther down the booking chain to later days. Having the courage of a strong conviction will drastically increase your chances of getting booked, especially if it's opposite the prevailing opinion(s).

We worked with a great expert and author who took the pro-cop story angle in the news based on his experience as a black police officer. Taking this stance at the time of his interview (#BLM) was not the racially expected position for him to carve out for himself. Frankly, it was both controversial and brave of him to do so, and it opened him up to numerous attacks. But because he was clearly representing his authentic beliefs, and staking out unexpected territory in the process, he received many bookings from shows looking for that position in the discussion.

Many experts are terrified to participate in a polarity discussion at a media event; however, it is my belief that proper on-camera training and a solid knowledge of your content creates all the necessary confidence to deliver an important and often very necessary message.

All of the experts should be ready and able to go on the *Howard Stern Show* or *Rush Limbaugh Show* at a moment's notice. That means being grounded deeply enough in their speaking points that they can handle anything. Practice your appearances on local media affiliates before jumping into the big leagues. The only way I got through being pranked by Sacha Baron Cohen was by remaining true to my content, i.e., my brand, my deck of cards, my speaking points, which in this case meant being a professional on-camera coach who is cool and calm under pressure. Of course, by not becoming reactive or flustered by his antics, I gave him a segment that wasn't as usable as it would have been if I'd made a fool of myself. Looking back, I'm glad I stuck to my content, even if it meant getting cut from his movie.

There's also a third position to take, a middle position, which we call the Voice of Reason (VOR). Often, by this day of breaking news, the Voice of Reason won't be invited to the table. However, we believe the Voice of Reason can be balanced in the polarity of the conversation. Expert VORs can still work if they have the parameters of their own content locked down. PERIOD! This is why we are big on-camera training thumpers. The opportunity is there, but you need to understand how to craft a position or argument that is within the integrity of your mission statement. You can be a VOR and still take a position.

On Day 4, if no new developments have surfaced, the story will now open up to related or kaleidoscope points of view. This doesn't necessarily require someone with a direct relation to the event or even a polarity of opinion. Just a voice who can help facilitate the question *What have we learned?* or *What can we learn?* conversations to begin opening up. This is where tangible practical tips are required, as well as overall perspective. If it's a fire, *Stop, Drop, and Roll* matters.

If it's Prince dying without a will, we want to make that relevant to the viewer's own life, i.e., "What three things do I need to have in order upon my death?" Simple pedantic information can get passed along here—how to draw up a will, a living directive, a transfer of assets, etc.

There is a golden opportunity in every story to share your part of the tale and to contribute to the collective story; however, demand, timing, and content are key. When you get booked, execution of the material will be what determines your rebooking.

This is why we coach our clients to ask themselves two questions when they're considering pitching themselves for a story:

1. What unique contribution can you make that adds value to the story?
2. How can you communicate your contribution most effectively?

At TVGuestpert, we call this contribution the "angle" from which experts can provide their respective expertise on most stories. I strongly encourage you to position yourself accordingly when trying to get bookings. I assure you, more than anything, producers are looking for fresh voices, fresh faces, and fresh angles.

A Word to Authors

Authors don't fit into the parameters of breaking news stories, so they need to find other ways to promote their books in the media. Authors don't often leave themselves at their best advantage when they call our office and say, "My book just came out and I am now ready to promote it."

When a book is published and the author hasn't started the promotion at least six months prior to the publishing date, it's like sending out invitations on the night of a party and wondering, *Where are all the guests?*

When my first book was published, it was through the conventional literary route. I spent months on the book proposal, twice as much time landing a deal and an agent in New York, and then I had to write the damn thing! Looking back, I realized I spent nearly two years working on the publisher's book proposal, answering a lot of sales and marketing questions. Clearly, they were looking to see what I was going to bring to the table. Specifically, they wanted to know if I was the kind of author who would bring book sales into the bookstores. I just wanted to write my book and I thought the publishers would do the rest. By the time it finally hit bookstores in 2006, it had taken four long years to go from idea to bookshelf.

If only I'd known then what I know now. After working as a publisher, I understand that when the books are placed on bookstore's shelves, those books are there on consignment. This means that the publisher is financially backing and floating every single store copy. If your book doesn't sell, the bookstore sends the book back to the publisher as a return. Now your publisher has paid over and then over again for your book: the printing, the shipping, and the return are all on their tab. If you ever wondered why they go through such an intense vetting process when they look at a manuscript and meet an author, or heavily promote their new celebrity book, wonder no more. Before publishers put a book on their release calendars, they want to know what you're bringing to the table in terms of promotion, sales and marketing, and now influence. Even if you are a whiz at winning publicity through your content, you may not have the support you need from traditional publishers, who are often short on time, money, and staff to reach your target audience. This is especially true if you're a first-time author.

I'm a big believer in starting at least six months ahead of your book's publishing date to properly promote your book. Think of this pre-publicity as building your media platform by promoting the content of your book as a buildup before a big media launch. That's been a huge part of our success in getting our clients to hit the *New York Times'* bestseller list: generating traffic and buzz before publication.

Building a newsletter database before your book comes out is a key component of pre-release book promotion. It definitely takes some traction to build up a database, which is yet another reason to start early. The efforts are worth it: that database can be transformed into your potential sales list once the book is published. This list also becomes an asset in reassuring national book sales managers who want to know that you can personally increase the traffic of the book.

Think of publishing a book like having a baby. Long before the baby arrives, you need to organize the baby's room, take a childbirth class, spread the news to your colleagues, organize a birth plan, tour the hospital, search for a pediatrician, buy a car seat, pack your hospital bag, pick up baby announcements, and … whew, I'm sure I've missed a few steps along the way. The point is that you don't start this whole process the day your baby is born. It's very important that everything you're doing to build your platform is happening while you're producing, writing, and editing your book. To do it when the book comes out is too late—it's like missing your own party. Or the birth of your own child!

About 95 percent of the time, authors begin their publicity right as the book is coming out. Publishers, meanwhile, are listing their books through publishing industry catalogs six months to two years in advance. Take advantage of this discrepancy! Be on the right side of this particular book ledger. While other authors are planning their book parties, you should get busy building up your television appearances, social media, and database. Trust me, your party will be a lot more fun if you know you've reached all the people necessary to buy your book ahead of time.

Wait! Are you wondering how you promote your book on television before the book even comes out? The answer is simple. Change your plug to "Upcoming Author of …" and direct traffic to your pre-sale book website, your website, your publisher's website, or B&N.com and Amazon.

CHAPTER 10

DON'T BLAME THE HOST!

The worst thing a guest or Guestpert can say to me after a taping is "The host didn't ask me x, y, and z." Even as a producer, to hear this as they walked off the stage was so disheartening. Why? Simple ... Because they should have been better prepared!

They had every opportunity to own their content. Both host and guest are mic'd for audio, which means each has an equal ability to communicate to the viewer. Furthermore, if it is a well-produced segment, the guest's content and speaking points have been preapproved by the producer. Do hosts have bad days? *Of course.*

Perhaps they didn't get the script until late and wound up reading it in bed right before crashing from exhaustion. Even when hosts do their homework, don't rely on the fact that they will read your book prior to your appearance. On most large shows, it is virtually impossible for a host to read the volume of material that's available.

We were lucky enough recently to welcome *The Doctors'* senior supervising producer, Shannon Hunt, as the guest producer at one of our TVOnCamera-Training.com workshops. Shannon shared that she gives her host, Travis Stork, pre-packets that could include as much as three hundred pages of medical research, supporting material, guest pre-interviews, and, of course, the script.

On a nationally syndicated talk show like that, a host may tape as many as six to nine shows per week. Think about that—producer packets for six tapings per week alone comes out to 1,800 pages a week. Throw in the guest's books that are often included along with the packets, and you're talking about a lot of material to absorb as the host of a show.

If the host doesn't give you a lead-in question or a prompt, it'll be on you to segue to the next speaking point right away. We discussed this already! Leave enough room for the host to lead, direct, and interject if so inclined; after all, the host is leading the tango; however, please give yourself permission to move the content forward. Lean into your content, don't wait it out.

I use the language of permission because in this choreographed tango, you don't ever want it to be a parent-child or teacher-student dance, where you are waiting for someone else to grant you permission. I'm not saying you should take over the lead, but you want to keep the dance a harmonic expression of two equals. We call these appearances interviews, which often gives guests the false impression that they should defer to the host on all prompts. But come on, wouldn't that make for a very boring dance to watch, or a limp dance partner at best?

Energy

All producers expect that their guests will have energy. What does having energy mean? During our TVOnCameraTraining.com workshops, I explain that having energy is the place inside your being where you feel like you are about to be weird for being too over-the-top.

Remember, your appearance needs to translate a) through a camera that is recording; b) up to a satellite in orbit in our planet's atmosphere; c) back down through a cable; and, finally, d) into a box—a television, computer, or smartphone. That's a lot of hoops for energy to *jump* through. I'm not asking anyone to turn into an overly caffeinated, Tom Cruise couch jumper. But I do want you to access an energy that goes beyond your normal voice or projection from the core of your being. It takes an inner energy to make those quantum projection leaps.

You know that you have this energy reserve if you are nervous, have butterflies in your stomach or you have to go to the bathroom to relieve yourself. These are the physical symptoms to acknowledge as a good thing, a positive sign that lets you know you have the energy reserve for the performance you are about to give.

In breaking up the tension of the moment, I will often joke with Guestperts before they go on that they are not allowed to go to the bathroom until after the appearance. After all, I remind them, relieving themselves might release the tension required for the most effective delivery required.

Some of our clients have been on television for serious news topics, and often they feel that the word *energy* is not appropriate for grave news topics such as plane crashes or school shootings. When producers ask for energy, they are not asking for happiness or excitement. What they want is the energy that comes from your *passion* for the topic as it relates to your expertise. Remember, your message has to penetrate a home already oversaturated with content. That's why energy or passion is so important to producers. They do not want a flatlined personality as a guest on their show. They do not want you too relaxed or overconfident either, as relaxation often translates to apathy on camera and overconfidence often translates to not being actually in the moment. Being nervous means you are in your body, ready to transmit. When I was a television producer and I heard from guests that they weren't nervous, I would get so nervous for them that I would want to throw up because I knew they did not have the energy necessary for maximum on-air impact.

There isn't much that happens with our Guestperts that we haven't heard before from our producing colleagues. Coming back to that "it's-a-small-world" thing: One time, while we were watching a client from our office during a live television appearance, a text came in from the producer: "Why isn't your client smiling?"

Indeed, I could see the deep, serious expression on my client's face as he was being introduced as if he were facing a firing squad instead of a peppy morning show. He of course was being framed with that beautiful, oh-so-serious face in a tight close-up. I could only look on helplessly as his expression grew grimmer and my phone blew up with texts from a frustrated and disappointed producer. Bottom line, this client did not possess the energy required for audience engagement and the producer knew it.

Fear and Intention

A few words about fear and intention. Do you want to sell widgets, save the world, or do you fall somewhere in between? Having a clearly formed intention will always help you stay focused and passionate when that red light goes on. So make sure you take the time to determine your intention before making an appearance. More than likely, you'll either be relaying information or promoting a great show, food, place, or product. If you find yourself getting lost or nervous, return to your intention. I encourage you to remind yourself, "You know what? This isn't about me ... this is about me being a vessel to share information in an entertaining way!" I promise the pressure will ease up almost immediately. You know all that energy that's coursing through your veins, turning in on you, and making you feel SO nervous? What it's actually saying is, "This isn't about me, this is about me being of service; this is about me taking this great information I have and sharing it with the world." Then think about pushing all that energy outward, to the people who need it most ... your audience!

Sometimes the best way to combat your fear is to face it head on. When I was making national appearances on QVC, each segment was performed live. On live TV, there are no second chances or multiple takes. On average, the segments ran about seven minutes, and I needed to sell a certain amount of product within those seven minutes or else the whole product would be taken off air. I'm telling you, it was a lot of pressure! But whenever I would start to feel that fear bubbling to the surface, I had a mantra I would say to myself: "Face it and embrace it!" Sure I felt scared. But really there are very few times in your life that you're given the opportunity to feel this alive. I didn't know if I was going to sink or swim, and that's exciting! Every single fiber of my being was alive in those moments, which I realized was a precious and rare gift.

Embrace your fear. Face it and move toward it. Fear is often a guidepost that signals you are heading in the right direction and growing into the person you were meant to be. It's an awesome life experience to experience fear and act anyway.

To risk failing and discover in the process a larger, more courageous version of yourself. How cool is that? Reframing nervousness as actually being excitement has really helped me and a lot of my clients deal with those on-camera jitters, even … or should I say especially … during live appearances.

Excited or Shut Down? Since it's such a common occurrence, let's take a little deeper look now at the skills necessary to tackle nervousness. Usually nervousness manifests in one of two ways:

1. You get jittery and your heart starts beating faster.
2. You get very subdued and withdrawn.

If you fall into the first category and are super excitable when you get nervous, practice doing visualizations. Picture yourself being calm, relaxed, and remaining that way until the end of your appearance. Some deep breathing exercises would be really great for this brand of nervousness; maybe try some stretching or yoga before you go on.

Advice to the second camp of nervous nellies is to visualize being engaged and energetic, and super dynamic on camera. For these types, some push-ups or jumping jacks, something to get their blood flowing is the order of the day, so that they're really present and dynamic in their appearance.

Know your nervousness, people. Figure out how you react to the stress of appearing on TV and then adjust from there!

"Yeah, but…"

"Yes, And," as Shannon says!

Sometimes you need to cut yourself some slack. There is nothing wrong with saying, "I don't know the answer to the question; however, what I can tell you is …" and resume the pivot to your next prescribed speaking points.

Try not to repeat speaking points. This is an easy fall-back habit to lean on. Unfortunately, it shows a lack of confidence in your content, and is inherently insulting the viewers since it offers them nothing new.

When confronted with a stumper of a question, two of my favorite polite pivots are:

1. "I don't know about that, but what I can tell you is …"
2. "In my experience, what I know is …"

Using the anchor's name is another great tactic that serves multiple purposes. It buys you a precious moment or two of thinking time to allow the next set of words to travel from your brain to your mouth. It also creates camaraderie and rapport with the anchor/host, establishing a type of familiarity that is always appreciated by the viewer. After all, the host is your dance partner!

It is important to re-contextualize your book without being too salesy, pushy, or promotional. Audiences smell this obnoxious odor a mile away and will quickly turn away or, worse, turn the channel!

Television producers have a cringe factor when an author says something like, "When you read my book, you'll learn ..."

They don't realize that this type of statement has basically just insulted the viewers. You're shaming them by saying in effect that they're wasting their time watching you on this show because what they really need to know is in your book.

Rather than sell the book, focus on selling your ability as an expert in the field to be of service. Books sell when the show is over and the viewers want more from the guest that they just watched. They're not buying your book because you told them to buy it, right? They're buying it because you said something valuable during your appearance, and they want more of that value in their lives!

When it comes to where to look on camera, it's important to remember that the perspectives and sight lines of hosts and experts are as different as their roles on the show.

I just watched *The Kitchen* on the Food Network, a show that features four core hosts. Two of them lead each cooking segment, while the other two play the role of the tasters. Since they are the established hosts of the show, they can and do frequently look at the camera to involve the home audience in their scrumptious tasting and enthusiasm for cooking.

Eye Contact

During a recent episode of *The Kitchen*, there was a guest appearance by author Kathy Freston, who was promoting her new cookbook, *Clean Protein*. Kathy Freston is known for her delicious vegan cookbooks. She is a highly respected television expert who's made numerous appearances over the course of her career. Appearing on *The Kitchen*, Kathy did what a great guest would do—she focused on the host and her cooking. She did *not* make eye contact with the camera or the home audience as she was a guest on the show, not the host. It was not her job to invite the home audience into the segment. Her job was to deliver her content and speaking points to the host, and by proxy, to the audience. Consequently, her appearance came off as natural, appealing, and entertaining as always.

As a guest and expert on a show, your focus needs to remain on the host and the topic at hand. You never want to break the audience sight line with a look off camera, which in turn makes them wonder, *What the heck are you looking at?* Even worse, when guests try to look at the camera, they'll hit the wrong camera, which is very disorienting to the home audience because it suddenly appears as if they are looking off into space. It is a distraction.

The good news is that not worrying about the camera makes the role of the guest expert easier. Just focus on the host and the camera will find you. You do not need to find the camera; therefore, simply remain present with your content and the experience at hand.

"What about when I'm introduced? Where do I look then?" The answer is still the same. As a guest, you look at the host. The camera will find your face. It is that simple.

Again, the good news is this is probably the easiest advice in the section to follow.

Camera Ready

At TVGuestpert, we require all of our clients to show up on set already hair and makeup ready. And, yes, that includes our male clients. There are a variety of reasons that we demand this. For one, we market our roster to producers as one stocked with camera-ready experts. We also firmly believe that experts who know how to take care of their own hair and makeup make themselves that much more attractive to producers—literally and figuratively.

The reality is, some shows do not have professional hair and makeup folks available. Other shows do, but only to provide touch-ups. We had one incident at a company where the show notified us ahead of time that they did, in fact, provide professional hair and makeup to all of their guests. Nevertheless, we held true to our own company policy in spite of this seemingly generous perk, and required our guest to pay for this service before she arrived at the studio.

On this particular morning, there was a major breaking news story. The 6 a.m. hour in which our guest was to appear wound up going through a major last-minute overhaul, or what producers call "restacking" the show. In this case, the producer frantically came into the green room looking for guests who were able to go on-air at a moment's notice. When she realized our client was camera-ready with professional broadcast hair and makeup for high-definition television, she put our guest on the air immediately. The other green room guest was not as fortunate. This aspiring expert, who was neither our client, nor camera-ready, was sent home for the day. The producer told me later that it would have taken too long to get that other client hair and makeup ready. They needed to be flexible with the show rundown that day in order to accommodate the breaking news story.

Our client, meanwhile, who had complained earlier about having to pay for professional broadcast hair and makeup for a show that provided this service, called later to thank us for mandating this standard of excellence. Because they sent the other guests home, my client was booked every hour from 6 a.m. to 10 a.m., thereby receiving an additional four bookings she would most certainly not have enjoyed otherwise.

In addition to professional makeup, what you wear is just as important. Bolder colors usually work better with women, particularly jeweled tones, which include rose, aqua, teal, garnet, and orange. Whenever possible, avoid black, white, yellow, and green. After receiving this advice, a lot of women will protest, "But Ellen wears white." True, that she does. But let's look a little deeper, shall we? Ellen's entire set is lit to light her. It is not lit to light you. Similarly, no set that you walk onto will be lit specifically for you. In general, white clothing throws off the lighting and color balance and can make your face and skin tone look green or yellow as a result. This is why you don't wear white on set. Unless your name is Ellen—and the entire set has been lit for you!

The truth is, stars receive different treatment than the rest of us. While I was co-executive producer at AMC's industry talk show, *Sunday Morning Shootout*, we had iconic legendary actress Shirley MacLaine on as a guest. She held up the entire production and insisted the lighting grip adjust a key light to her framing. I was blown away. I had never seen anyone else ask for or receive this special treatment. Shirley MacLaine, my exec producer explained, apparently does this on all her guest appearances. Shirley, I might add, like Ellen, has earned the right to do so.

The reason green should be avoided on camera is because shows often employ the use of a green screen. Usually you'll be informed about a green screen shoot prior to the booking; however, it is a good practice not to include green items in your on-camera wardrobe. A green screen is what the weather reporters use as a background so that a computer can generate the mapping that goes behind them. The actual mapping you see as a viewer at home does not exist behind the on-air weatherperson, who is simply making the gestures to the green screen by looking at an off-camera monitor. Green screens are used as a simple way for productions to create all sorts of scenic backgrounds. These background inserts can superimpose a practically infinite number of scenic possibilities, from outer space to the Hollywood sign. All while the talent stands directly in front of the green screen. If your wardrobe is green, the mapping will show up on you, giving you a floating-head-like appearance in the shot. Definitely not what we're going for on any booking!

Many women like to arm-wrestle me into letting them wear black because they look good in black. I'll admit that black has become a more acceptable color to wear on television. My feeling is if you are going to participate in the visual medium of television, then being void of color is counterproductive in a medium that rewards shining and being seen. Many traditional producers will tell you as well that they are not a fan of a guest wearing black.

Men and women both would do well to stay away from wearing clothing with small patterns like pinstripes or herringbone, which tend to "crawl" on screen and become distracting.

Accessories can add a touch and personal sparkle, but they require restraint and discernment to wear. Remember, where accessories are concerned, less is more. Don't wear anything that competes with your face, such as large earrings or oversized necklaces. Keep busyness, such as scarves and hair pieces, to a minimum. Be mindful that your bracelets don't create noise, and that necklaces and pins don't rub up against the lavalier or lapel microphone.

As a producer, I would always ask guests to remove their hats. So please leave your hats at home, unless you are a rapper on *Late Night* and you need it for your branding or edge. You'd better watch out for hats with logos on them. Those ubiquitous Kangol hats can create an ad sales conflict of interest (and giant headache) for a network when guests wear them on a popular show. Which makes the overall rule of thumb with hats simple and clean: they're another no-no!

For men, dark suits may look good in a business meeting, but they can cause the wearer to get lost on camera, especially if the backdrop is dark. We suggest our male clients wear a light blue shirt underneath the suit. I recommend wearing suits in the blue or chocolate family for appearances.

Remember to take the gum out of your mouth before you walk on set. I cannot tell you how many on-camera guests have had to spit out their gum or mints into my hand right before showtime. Yuck!

Bring more than one outfit or shirt to the shoot. Even if you think the one you picked out is cute, producers don't want guests with outfits that match their hosts, or the outfit of the guest who appeared on the show right before you. A good practice is to always bring extra outfits for the producers to decide. You never know when the occasional nerves might precipitate a spilled cup of coffee right before a taping. Trust me, there aren't enough napkins or club soda to sort that out!

Women, sit at an angle in your chair with your feet crossed at the ankles to give your body shape, and be careful to never sit all the way back in your chair no matter how comfy the chair looks.

Men, please don't ride a horse when sitting on set. Manspreading doesn't work on the subway, or on camera. Trust me, that is not a flattering view to present to the home audience. Enough said on that!

CHAPTER 11

THE GREEN ROOM

Everything that goes down in the green room before the show is as important as all the moments leading up to it. The green room is the calm, cool, collected place where you wait before you go on set and on air.

Call Time

Call time is the pre-arranged time to meet at the studio in which you'll be taken to the green room to wait before your go on set. The call time is specific. Being a guest that arrives too early can often run into a lack or limitation of green room space that is booked for other guests who have earlier call times and taping times. Sit in your car if you are early. Naturally, it goes without saying what the unspoken consequences are for being late for a call time.

Over the summer, I sat with our financial Guestpert for Twentieth Television's daytime talker called *The Daily Helpline* backstage in the green room. Our call time was 8:00 a.m. Tape time was scheduled for 9:00 a.m. Our Guestpert had asked us the night before if we thought he'd be back in the office for a noon appointment. We thought possibly, but you never know. We walked out of the studio at 11:45 a.m. Yikes! I'm happy to report that he made it back to his office in time, but I'm even happier that he never said a word to the producers about his conflicting obligation.

Moral of the story is, you want to make sure you're the easiest person the show will be dealing with all day. That means being ready to go on camera the second you arrive on set, and doing your best to be free the rest of the day. And that if you DO have a later commitment that you can't get out of, keep it to yourself, or at least to your coaches at TVGuestpert! Always remember that anything can happen—and often does—to throw off the day's shooting schedule.

On the front end, another guest may be running late or needing extra time in hair and makeup. You, on the other EASIER hand, can keep the shoot on schedule by being able to tape your segment early. I've also seen plenty of shoots running behind when the other guest is an A-list actor who is giving the producer a hard time because she has to get to a movie premiere. Yes, your time is valuable and in demand. But you don't want to let your ego get in the way in these cases. I'm sorry, but there is no real value in presenting yourself as an in-demand commodity. Producers will simply release you and move on. There's far greater value in being able to say, "Not a problem. I don't mind waiting in the green room a bit longer. We can tape my segment after they're finished."

Trust me, these are tense moments. The green room is where everyone has to sit in their nerves before being called to set.

If you're ready to go right away, or can be flexible if segments need to be switched (as in the above example) and yours ends up taping an hour later, what do you think that makes you? You've become the solution to the producer's problem! Even though producers tend to see guests as being interchangeable, making their day easier is something that will help you stand out and ensure that you get asked back. Need I remind you, producers go from show to show to show and take their contact list of valuable assets with them. So let's make sure you stay on that list!

Mic'd

Once you're in the studio, assume anything you say can be heard by anyone at any given time. This is especially true after you've been mic'd, but it's even true when you're talking to someone on the production staff, who could just as easily be wearing a mic capable of recording anybody anytime. I can't count the number of stories I've heard (including some I've witnessed) where people on set think they're sharing an intimate moment with someone else that can easily be broadcast to everyone back in the control room, and sometimes throughout the set.

Donald Trump's conversation with Billy Bush on the set of *Extra* was not private in the way that he thought. Everything you say can and will be used against you.

Many of these stories have a certain degree of humor to them, but not all. The most dramatic I've heard involved a young expert on his first appearance. He had called his friends on his cell phone and was bragging about how great the feeling of being on the set was for him. The problem was that he was making up lies about members of the crew and saying crass things about the women in particular. He was asked to leave the set without a taping. Don't let this happen to you unless you want your segment to be cancelled and to never be asked back.

> **Expert Tip:** *If you've been mic'd and you have the desire and time to use the restroom before your segment tapes, that's an appropriate situation to ask whether or not your mic is on and if it can be turned off. Other than that, assume anyone on set can and will hear everything you're doing and/or saying.*

Release Forms

When in the green room you'll also be asked to sign a release if you haven't done so already. It's a standard form, and at that point the only classy thing to do is sign it right away. Please become familiar with them prior to the taping. Yes, you are signing all promotional rights away. That shouldn't be a problem for you if you are in command of your content. Live news shows don't require a release form. Although there's no way around signing it, if you have any questions, comments, or concerns, ask the producer to email you a copy during the pre-interview phase so you can review it and ask questions if need be. Although the language and the content should both be pretty universal and straightforward, you should also ask your representation (legal, talent, publicist, etc.) any questions you may have prior to your appearance. Keep in mind, it's the same form everyone is expected to sign. Making it more of a process than it needs to be will only serve to frustrate the production staff, thereby turning you into someone they don't like working with. And frankly, if you do have any reservations, waiting until signing time in the green room is already too late. All taped shows will require release forms. Ask for it before you come to the set.

We believe all bookings are good bookings. Even the smallest, most seemingly insignificant appearances will give you an opportunity to work new content. And you never know who is watching. You are also creating a relationship with a producer. We see no drawback in accepting a booking. If something comes your way that you're completely wrong for, chances are you won't be asked or seriously considered anyway. We have this expression at the office, "It's always a yes until it is a no." Another one I use often with my clients is "Take yes for an answer!" Stay open to possibilities, even if they seem out of your comfort zone or your exact line of content. Although you hope to be Dr. Phil's expert of choice on your given topic, it's a long way to the top and a longer way to a consistent top. Even when you get booked on a local show in the smallest market in the country, that content can get picked up by affiliates and run throughout the country. No opportunity should be too big or too small.

Please try and stay as open-minded as possible when it comes to opportunity. We booked a client once on a small affiliate spot that wound up running on all major networks. Point is, you just never know. If your segment is particularly funny, insightful, or entertaining, it could be posted online and find a whole new audience there. Even if the audience isn't a massive or an especially mainstream one, your content might make its way to a series of forums or Facebook pages relating to your topic, which might then help you gain a potentially global and instant audience of people interested in your book, site, etc. Which brings us back to why it's so important to have the correct video monitoring service in high resolution—assuming you want to make the correct sort of video copy that will help you maximize your content to its greatest potential.

Video Monitoring

Many times following an appearance, Guestperts use a website link to the show site for their own website. Links to third-party sites that you have no control of are not acceptable, because they are not providing an easy way for your followers to find them and may not stay active. Asking a producer for a copy of the show can be disastrous. The importance of having a video monitoring service cannot be overstated. There really is no better way to ensure your appearance is recorded in the right format and that you'll have it forever. The mistake many on-camera experts make is that they confuse a link sent by the producer as a file. A link is hosted directly on the show's website. This is finite and out of your hands. Which is why we require our Guestperts to acquire their appearance through a video monitoring service. This guarantees that they own the video file and can use it to edit into their demo reels, or to post on YouTube or their own website. They have control of the video file in perpetuity.

The other issue is that clients will hound a producer for a copy of the show or an updated link, which winds up disrupting the booking process. The producer now has to tap one of his dozen or so teammates in post-production or master control as a favor to get you a link. While waiting for this cumbersome task to be completed, he will dodge your calls because he doesn't have an answer for you yet. FYI: We don't want a producer to dodge your calls, or our calls for that matter, simply because you hounded him for a link of your appearance. In the old days, we would have sent a DVD copy of your show, but in modern lingo, it's now a file.

Aggregate your content properly so you can leverage these opportunities appropriately.

The Business of Platform Building

Platform building and creating a bridge from expert into the role of influencer requires acquiring media and then leveraging the exposure on social media as influencer. The primary purpose for getting an expert exposure in the media is to build a platform from which you can leverage larger opportunities.

We are sitting down for a meeting with a soon-to-be-published author through TVGuestpert Publishing. We lay out all of his platform pieces on the table in order to strategize where the strengths and weaknesses are.

We look at his website. We review his data capture. We study his mailing list. We compare his social media output through LinkedIn, Twitter, Instagram, and Facebook. We examine his social media following. We look at his personal Facebook page. We look at his YouTube following. We plug his name into Google to see what comes up about him. We watch his prior television appearances. We subscribe to his newsletter. We review his headshots. What is his imaging? What is his messaging? What story is he telling? Are his communication systems connected up from website to social media so that he can make announcements swiftly? Is the branding and messaging congruent across platforms?

YOUR HEADSHOTS

Expert headshots are a different flavor than host headshots. They need to reflect professional maturity with media savviness. They need to be captivating. We want to see your whole face in proportion to the frame without headroom. Remember these need to work for television and not just your job. In a digital communication world, your headshot in an email is going to be the first visual cue as to whether the producer will want to book you before they review any of your content and demo reel.

Platform building is the layering up of relevant branding and messaging to create the next platform piece in order to leverage the next opportunity.

The millennial generation has a knack for social media communication that more mature experts often don't.

When Guestpert clients have a television booking, they know to pre-announce the upcoming appearance through social media, blogs, websites, and newsletters. We call this the Bang for the Buck Number 1. If you have fun with this, it can be a "Countdown To" type of event. An example: Only seventeen days left until Jacquie sits down with Oprah! (Don't be afraid to dream big.) Then comes Bang for the Buck No. 2, aka the Don't Miss announcement, which is unveiled on the day of the shoot and should feature a classic shot of you in full regal hair and makeup. Rinse, repeat, then post to your social platforms. Another fun thing some of our Guestperts do is record a Facebook Live as they pull onto the studio lot for their appearance. Bang for the Buck No. 3 is the photo shoot with the host or signage from the set. Bang for the Buck No. 4 is making sure everyone has the air date or the playback. This can come via all sorts of announcements in the systems setup through platform building. The final Bang for the Buck, No. 5, involves using the last appearance to broker and leverage your next appearance on an even larger scale.

Enough Bang for the Buck can lead to Buck for the Buck; let's find out how! Which leads into the social media space and the role of the influencer—whether you are an expert or simply want to be just an influencer, a new space in a new frontier!

HOW TO LEVERAGE YOUR MEDIA APPEARANCES

Leverage 1 – Write about it:

Pat Pattison's article was featured in this week's PBS's Next Ave., which receives over 500,000 unique users a month of Pat's ideal audience for clients and for generating more clients.

Leverage 2 – Apply the media success to your core business and supplementary vehicles:

Pat Pattison is a certified executive and transition coach. He is also co-founder of The Incentive Plus Network (now a division of Cross MediaWorks) and is producing and hosting "Remade in California," in cooperation with the State of California Community Colleges.

Leverage 3 – Lock in next appearance to promote your message:

Pat's next interview is already on the calendar for ABC's morning show Sac & Co, on September 1, where Pat will be discussing hot topic "Remade in California—Community Colleges Are the New Hot Zone for Mid-Life Retraining."

Leverage 4 – Set up development meetings to discuss business expansion and plan:

TVGuestpert has 4 p.m. call with national cable company tomorrow, Thursday, August 27, to discuss opportunities with Pat Pattison's platform.

Leverage 5 – Mailing List & Social Media:

Send out your featured appearance to your mailing list of 8,000+ people, as well as posting on all your social media platforms.

Leverage 6 – Update all your materials:

Demo reel, website, etc. with your best sound bites, appearances, and quotes for your next round of bookings and meetings. Work on your book.

ACT 3: INFLUENCERS

CHAPTER 12

THE VALUE OF BEING AN INFLUENCER

To some, the world of social media can be considered a huge undertaking. For many business owners, social media is another chore on an already infinite task list to execute during the day keeping one focused on working in the business instead of on the business.

Questions like: How do you monetize social media? How do you get more followers? How do you stand out as a unique figure with an abundant amount of profiles and personalities to scroll through? These are huge questions for experts, celebrity brands, and hosts! And what if you only want to be an influencer, not a host or an expert? How do you leverage social media to get a television deal or attract more clients to your business?

As with all good things that take time and cultivation, navigating your way around the social media world can prove to be beneficial. This means you need to familiarize yourself with the history, lingo, and trends found in social media; and that's exactly what we're going to start off with before Shannon and I spill all our tips and tricks to becoming a prominent social media influencer. Becoming a prominent social media figure can help expand your branches of expertise in places you never knew existed, cultivating an influence you didn't know you had access to.

Google +, Facebook, and Twitter paved the way to becoming not only more interconnected with each other in society, but more organized. What's more important to note are the connections that all these platforms have with each other (just in case you're wondering why your recent post didn't get as many likes as you initially anticipated). Google owns YouTube, Facebook owns Instagram, and yet each is used for something completely specific. Facebook, the largest platform, is seen well utilized among the older generation to connect with friends and family and not so much as a platform to place content for followers. Twitter is primarily used for opinion and breaking news cycles—a compacted site to share your thoughts and feelings regarding a topic. And last, but definitely not least, Instagram can be seen as the place for everything and anything lifestyle.

We have just scratched the surface of these new and changing trends, but when all three of these social media giants are used efficiently and effectively, you'll have a rock-solid foundation.

There are five social media platforms that we will focus on here for review, even though there are many others. Some of these others, have also, already disappeared, remember Myspace?

FACEBOOK: Survived the post-Myspace apocalypse to become one of the most popular international social media platforms. The interesting dynamic to note is that once the whole family tree got on and joined Facebook, the youth, who originally activated Facebook, disappeared. Why? No teenager wanted to show off to their friends while their grandmother in Missouri was "following" them. The mass exodus of the youth demographic migrated to Instagram and Snapchat.

The good news about Facebook is that the mature demographic enjoyed being connected on Facebook as a social media platform resurrecting friends from all walks of their life. As a result, Facebook is a remarkably viable option for social media for an older demographic who is loyal to this platform. Just don't expect to find teenagers in this space often.

Facebook is changing its momentum toward being a video platform service to compete with YouTube, making the need for clarity of branding, messaging, and on-camera training significantly important.

TWITTER: Twitter is the drop and run social media platform for up to the moment opinions. If you are watching the Superbowl, Twitter is the place to share your very own play-by-play comments to your followers on the game as it unfolds.

For us at TVGuestpert, we work and follow many journalists who use this platform. They share up to the moment feedback about breaking news and other stories that they are working on.

Just take a look at the analysts on our nightly news segments. Television critics actively support their conversations and expertise through the use of Twitter. It has now become a major basis for what journalists and scientists call "evidence." Once President Donald Trump tweets that tweet, it's out in the universe forever because the analysts already showcased it on their green screen behind them on television.

LINKEDIN: This is the professional social media platform. The branding on LinkedIn, in my opinion, needs to be the most professional, non-personal, not casual, of all the social media platforms. This is the place for A game performances. The encouragement here is to post on LinkedIn messaging, branding, and videos that are specific to your job, work, business, or professional expertise. Family vacation photos should not show up on your feed here. If you take away anything from Act 3, not all postings on all platforms are the same.

YOUTUBE: A video social media platform that has subscribers instead of followers. Facebook is looking to compete with YouTube as a video social media platform, but YouTube has the market on this and is churning out YouTube celebrities who are paid handsomely by the droves that would put reality television show stars to pasture. Instagram uses stories and now their IGTV to try and play in the YouTube ballpark. Consider the influence of YouTube by the mere fact that songs like Coldplay's "Hymn for the Weekend" or Eminem's "Love the Way You Lie" can have a billion plus views on one music video. Viewers on YouTube are not only unique views, but also repeated views. Television and film do not generate views that large, making the power of audiences on YouTube powerful. How does this tie into the smaller YouTube celebrity? Stay tuned ... as Shannon breaks down the power of the nano, micro, and macro influencer.

INSTAGRAM: Last, but certainly not least is Instagram. This is deliberately mentioned last as it is probably the most significant platform for being an influencer. It's a lifestyle platform where the art of storytelling is very specific and should be strategic. It's where messaging has the ability to create a call to action which is important for marketing. It's where the head count of followers matters to companies who are willing to pay.

In following Gal Gadot of *Wonder Woman* and her heroic rise to Instagram success, I noted that most of her posts contain that coveted inscription below her name. It is often written as a social media influencer's favorite words. Looking at her latest post as I write this, I see the words "Paid partnership with Reebok" above a photo of her in the gym, reflecting back on the year 2018. On another day, she is seen posing front-face to the camera with a bold lip color, sporting her "Paid partnership with Revlon." This photo quantified to approximately 1,546,429 likes, not including any reposts or shares. Other celebrities such as Reese Witherspoon and Jennifer Garner have a few "paid partnerships" with other major businesses and brands, but not monetizing at the frequency that Gal Gadot is earning. Not every celebrity has that kind of influence, yet it is every influencer's dream and the game that everyone wants in on.

As a *New York Times* bestselling publisher, TVGuestpert has had celebrities on occasion post a product for our Guestperts. Congratulations to Christy Whitman's The Enlightened Kid Program, which earned a shout-out from television's very own supermodel and TV Personality Chrissy Teigen. Looks like John Legend not only has to watch out for his badass wife, but his future badass kid, as well. This post influenced our author's project and created more awareness of her brand outside of her own reach.

From my perspective as a storyteller, I want to know what *your* story is. Whether you feel more comfortable using Twitter, Facebook, or Instagram, there is always a narrative. The dimensions of the story you want to tell can encompass a great deal of things, such as what it is that you are willing to tell or share, and what it is that you want to keep private. Because if you ever get to Gal Gadot's scale of fame and success, it's best to know now that privacy will be hard to come by, but it will be easier to maintain if you already know the story you're here to tell and where it's appropriate to tell said story.

The boundaries of the story that many people share in their own personal media include faces of family and friends, animals, food, adventures, and the occasional work crossover post. On another note, identify how far you want to be intimate with your audience. As a professional, you may not want people to know where you live or what that looks like, even if it is on your personal social media account. And unless your brand follows a specific kind of activism, it's best to stay away from commenting on the latest political or religious controversy occurring somewhere in the world. It adds a certain dimension to your audience, which could be either good or bad depending on your niche. Engaging in very heated or polarizing conversations can actually limit further growth in your social media landscape if what you're saying or engaging in does not align with your own personal brand. This, however, doesn't need to be the case for everyone. How, then, can we become a voice when it seems like we're in a world of information coming at us from every angle imaginable?

It was only ten years ago that you could easily sweep a negative story about your company under the rug. This is no longer the case. Whatever you post in the virtual reality space will be there ... practically forever. We take this into consideration when we work with our clients. It's important to make sure, now more than ever, that their messaging on any platform is what they mean to say. "Say what you mean, mean what you say, but don't say it mean" is a golden rule to live by in this increasingly growing technological era.

The use of video doesn't have to be as formal as a television appearance, but the same rules apply for making credible, respectable and meaningful videos. In the case of social media versus television, when it comes to video, television appearances are like job interviews while social media videos are more like having dinner at a friend's house. One environment may be less formal than the other, but the same manners still apply.

Another tip to make the recipe smoother is to slice and dice: choose an angle that cuts the clutter. One of the biggest failures of messaging that we witness as a media development company is that companies only want to talk about "what they do." We've already talked about how it's important to plug in why you're here and what you do, but like the great Maya Angelou once said: "Everything needs to be done in moderation, even moderation itself."

Knowing your audience and knowing your customers are actually two different topics that should be experienced differently, too. That cliché "never judge a book by its cover" reigns true in most scenarios. Many businesses and entrepreneurs miss out on an abundant amount of media opportunity because they don't recognize the value in speaking to anyone who isn't a potential customer in the ROI business model. To gain optimal results, branching out to different audiences can provide new brand recognition that will translate to customer cash down the road. This is how social media platforms can be applied. Different media outlets provide access to different audiences that possess different mind-sets, the same as social media platforms. And if just one of those individuals likes what she sees from you, you're a shoo-in to a whole different community. Reaching these audiences allows for a collective consciousness disrupter. Just remember that it isn't all about the money.

How To Build An Influencer Studio At Home:

Here's a list of all the tools I have and recommend for at home use. Having your own equipment will set you up for success as a host, actor, TV personality, influencer, expert and more!

CAMERA: Canon XLR with both an audio input AND output. It's the only way to hear how your sound is while you're recording. I have a 60D camera, and although I love the camera the output is the one thing that it is lacking. Sony also makes a good camera in the Sony Handycam AX100 (or better). But let's also be real honest, if you have a 4K camera like an iPhone XR (or better), you are going to be doing pretty well with your image quality. Cameras just also have the ability to handle pro audio equipment, which is important when doing videos. Anyone who works in the technical side of tv/film will tell you if you want something to really seem pro, audio is key (although the gritty natural quality from a phone is super popular, at least right now, in the influencer space).

TAKSTAR SGC598 SHOTGUN MIC: This is a great affordable shotgun mic that really gets the job done if you need better sound than what the camera can pick up. Rode is probably the best mic out there, but I like this one a lot for a cheaper price point.

INTERACTIVEMEDIA.NET, TELEPROMPTER SET-UP WITH IPAD: If you are doing an online course, do instructional/educational content, or just have a lot of information you want to relay and don't want to forget key points, a teleprompter is a must. And now that they have teleprompter set-ups with iPads, it is so affordable. I got this set-up for $260, not including the iPad.

ALBOTT 70 INCH TRIPODS: You want to make sure your tripod is going to be tall enough when you need it to be and not so flimsy you are afraid to put your equipment on it. There are tons of tripods out there that are super cheap and don't extend high enough for anyone of normal height to do standup content when necessary. This is a really good option.

SENNHEISER EW 100 LAV KIT: Sennheiser is the best lavalier audio equipment. Period. It's also pricey, but worth it. I don't even mess around with less expensive brands. If you do some research, you can also find gently used kits on eBay or Craigslist. Don't go to anything older in version than EW 100.

NEEWER 700W LIGHTING KIT: This lighting kit is a great deal! You can just search this kit online and get it for $70, which includes the lights and a great case.

EOCEAN SELFIE TRIPOD STICK W/BLUETOOTH REMOTE: This selfie stick extends out to a full size tripod! I make all my clients get this for self-tapes (auditions you have to record on your own and send in) as well as to practice in between our coaching sessions. This is also great if you want to create video content on your phone. You can get your shot set up, put your phone in the selfie stick, and then grab the remote that has it's own little home at the bottom of the stick. The remote is linked via Bluetooth to your phone so you can press the record button from your remote and it will start and stop the video recording from wherever you have positioned yourself for the shot. This is only $20 on Amazon. A must have!

CHAPTER 13

THE NANO, MICRO, MACRO INFLUENCER

There are multiple influencers in the spectrum: a nano-influencer, micro-influencer, and macro-influencer, and within each of these influencers' world lies a completely different world from the next influencer. A nano-influencer is typically an individual with 1,000 to 5,000 followers. A micro-influencer is someone with 5,000 to 100,000 followers, and finally, a macro-influencer is typically seen as someone with 250,000 followers or more. Without all these components, or individuals, there would be no need for a platform to expand what you know best. Influencers who have reached celebrity status are marked at around five to seven million followers, more or less. They, however, are in a completely different realm and can only be taken into consideration when we look deeper into the world of social media and branding.

What does it even mean to be in these categories? Simply speaking, each of these influencers has a different door set out for them to walk through. The number of followers you have will determine the different types of endorsement opportunities that brands and businesses will offer you. As people first dipped their toes in these social media advertising waters, celebrities were practically the only people sought out for paid campaigns, which was usually done in tandem with our physical reality through posters, television advertisements, etc. Approaches change as social media has evolved, and brands and businesses have finally come to terms with the endless advertising possibilities that social media has to offer them that would be unwise to ignore. Why hire a celebrity to endorse their product or service for millions of dollars when there's a perfectly capable "instafamous" gal for a fraction of the price who can don that pretty two-piece clothing set or show off how she was able to gain those pearly white teeth?

There's no doubt that having a celebrity endorse a product will reach millions—if not billions—of people worldwide. Exposure, exposure, exposure. That is the name of the game. Nowadays, brands and businesses are genuinely curious about just how successful their product is and can be. Micro-influencers can help a lot with this. Though their scope is quite large, it is still small enough to engage with their fan base through comments and videos of personal testimonials. The best part about having one of these instafamous influencers sporting your product is the fact that they don't cost nearly as much as having Kim Kardashian glittering and glowing in that same two-piece outfit. Companies can monitor the engagement, watch conversations happening about the products, and save some major advertising dollars by paying a few hundred for a post versus thousands, hundreds of thousands, or even more for a celebrity post. Even with these celebrity posts and micro- or macro-influencers, there is still space for the nano-influencer. Free products are often given to these individuals in exchange for a free product post, which can help both the company and the endorser increase their following. It's a win-win situation!

Yes, companies save thousands, hundreds of thousands, and even in some cases millions of dollars using these nano- and micro-influencers. When working with an unrepresented nano- or micro-influencer where a product trade or post fee is set without any contracts, companies are only able to send out guidelines, website links, handles, and hashtags that need to be included for an online surfer to find their product. The influencers in this case have a ton of creative control over what they do with what they receive. Ownership is a completely different ball game in the influencer world, because influencers can in some situations legally claim complete ownership over the content if it turns out better than expected, whereas with a celebrity post where a lengthy contract is involved (or a micro/macro post with contract in place), ownership content will always belong to the advertisers. That's right. Read the contract.

Blair Taylor, president of Taylor Talent Services, who has worked in the entertainment industry representing commercial actors, models, and spokespeople for product-related work for over two decades, says about this unprecedented phenomenon of the celebrity influencer, "You can get access to an audience and a perspective. The Kardashians have millions of followers ... if you think one of them is cool, anything they use as a product is automatically cool."

Taylor describes the difference between these powerhouse celebrity influencers and other young influencers, who are "followed by a younger demographic, and those are the people that are still developing their buying habits. By the time you are 35–40, you have decided what you like ... you don't really have influencers in their 50s and 60s because the people in their 50–60s who would be following them already know what they like to buy and aren't as easily influenced. Another reason is because the technology is changing so rapidly. When you are younger, you are still trying to keep up and stay on trend. Micro-influencers are more eager, will work hard, and it's more trackable than celebrities ... [but they] need to treat it like a job and tend their garden every day if they want to be a player in that world and monetize their social media presence."

It's all about having that fire in your belly, isn't it?

Taylor also talked about one of his experiences that truly exemplified the changing trends in social media. He conducted a two-Instagram-post deal a few years ago for a supermodel advertising a Japanese eyeliner. The only requirement was to smile and look pretty with the product in hand. He says at the time when he did this, the posts were spaced four weeks apart and the model received only $150,000. That may seem like a lot, but Taylor pointed out that for a supermodel with nine million followers, if they had known back then the trends on content, the time of day things should be posted and how often, and how to really track the progress, that $150,000 investment they made on her could have had a huge return of profit and could have been a great deal for them. Not that it was a bad deal, but the results could have been maximized. The data and algorithms count, and they count bucks!

Taylor urges us to see the many options available to us: "Let's put this in perspective. If you buy advertising time on any daytime talk show, which can get millions of views, it costs hundreds of thousands of dollars. Imagine putting that few hundred thousand dollars and instead of reaching the one million viewers who watch that show, you can advertise through an influencer and reach ten million people."

It seems like we spun back in time to the Wild West. Only now it's a showdown between old (broadcast TV) versus new (social media).

Yet, the question will always remain: what is the best path for brands, businesses, or in this case—*you*—to take? Well, to be honest, it's really up in the air right now, as some people prefer the good old-fashioned way of making your dreams come true to the new-world way of doing things. Technology is still advancing, so keeping up with trends will only make your head spin. Again, remember Myspace? But for now, it appears that a multi-prong approach of leveraging is the best way to go and the popular game plan for most brands trying to get the word out about their product or services.

If funds allow, having a celebrity endorse your product, enlisting a few micro-influencers to rave about their wonderful transformations for a fixed fee, and even getting some cheap or free exposure from those nano-influencers seems to be the winning lotto ticket. Exhausting all your efforts will ensure your product is seen from all corners of the social media world and hopefully, in all corners of this no longer black-and-white world. Did you know the word "influencer" is still flagged on spell check as a typo? At least it was at the time this book was written. That's just how fast times change.

In researching this book, I had the opportunity to sit down to lunch with a top talent agent from one of the top three talent agencies here in Los Angeles and a top talent manager at one of the five biggest management firms to the stars. Yes—to those names on those stars you can find on Hollywood Boulevard. Both of these individuals are in the unscripted or alternative programming departments at their companies, and like many of these departments, there is now an influencer division in an effort to maximize the opportunities that might be available to clients. Their clients have to have at least around 750,000 followers or subscribers to even begin working with them! Unfortunately, I'm not able to tell you the names of these individuals and agencies, but what I can tell you from my hour interview with both of these talent representatives is that these are strange and confusing times we're living in.

Brands can now reach out to influencers with huge brand alignment deals, offer on-camera roles at huge networks or digital platforms, and even collaborate with major companies to invent and put their names on products. At this lunch we spent some time talking about what exactly sells on social media and how they spend their time tracking down the latest child yodeler who went viral so they can represent him for six months and see what kind of brand alignment deals or network opportunities they can get him. I mean, the "Damn Daniel" star sensation was on Ellen within a week and like with all waves, died down pretty fast after that. Or how about the "Laughing Chewbacca Mask Lady" who had a Mattel Barbie Doll made of her within one week. You have to strike while the iron's hot and see what traction you can get from these viral sensations.

The point is that social media and viral marketing have turned how we consume content on its head and we are still swirling with how to navigate these new waters. We know that influencers are targeted by brands to endorse their products because they engage and have influence within a particular community. Marketers and advertisers offer these product alignment and endorsement deals to pour their ad dollars into a space without having to create that audience for themselves. An established credible influencer with such an audience is the perfect ingredient to achieve the aspired outcome. It is a great avenue for them to circumvent the process of creating and establishing rapport with groups of people.

The crazy part about all this is that we still can't fully comprehend the social media world. People within the entertainment industry can't even agree on whether or not they should call these people influencers, expert influencers, or creators. And don't forget to take into consideration that there is also a world of YouTubers out there who specifically go by the term YouTubers—right, gamer #PewDiePie with your billion hits?

We're here to create and develop your skills and expertise and give you as much knowledge as possible in this ever-changing social media atmosphere, so that not only can you go viral like that child yodeler, but actually ride from one wave to another. In other words, have substance that can sustain you. We've already done our research. The first step in tying in your passion to social media is to first and foremost find your niche. Up until this point you have called your niche your expertise.

CHAPTER 14

FROM EXPERTISE TO NICHE

From camera roll to phone screen, Instagram is the thriving hub of sharing and viewing photos from all over the world. A quick visit to a page will provide an inside look at a company's brand, celebrity festivities, or just an everyday person meandering about her day. It's true what they say: a picture *really* is worth a thousand words.

Where we expect storytelling to go on social media platforms and as a service we provide through TVGuestpert is the concept of sharing micro-movies instead of just moment to moment captures. This means that future branding on social media will be preconceived in advance to tell a certain story over a period of time to specifically engage the viewer, and the content is cut or edited into micro stories to hold the daily attention and engagement while rolling out a storyline.

Enhancing one of the best, or worst, guilty pleasures to exist on social media is the increase of your followers to your pages. Sure, there are people that say *don't get upset about how many followers, likes, or comments you have.* And that's perfectly reasonable and understandable, but when you want to showcase your expertise and see that people are genuinely interested in what you have to say and offer, those things kind of do matter. They show that there's something unique about you and that people are really looking to your page for advice on a better life. This is where the catch is. By now, you have been bombarded with tons of facts not only about social media, but also about on-camera time cues, content, body language, and much more. There is one thing you need before you hit the ground running: your message and story.

Let's take what we learned from the earlier chapters of this book. We prepped you for your on-camera appearance, but why? Simply speaking, you were seen as someone who can help a producer with a segment on a certain topic—*a certain expertise.* You're an individual who knows practically everything and anything about your topic. Your niche is the very same thing you will be asked to talk about on your future (and hopefully successful) television appearance. Use the social media platform to express a larger story than just sharing a photo of a cup of coffee you are drinking that afternoon.

We can take all the terms we learned and tailor them to what it would look like in the social media world. Your opening sound bite would very much be considered those little videos simply introducing yourself to whoever comes across your page. A great tip would be to post these "opening sound bites" methodically, introducing a little fact about you as your presence and platform grows. Take-home information is of you talking about any tips you have for the day, what your product is about, or anything you want your audience to know. This could be captured in a photo and further explained through your caption or for Twitter users, through your tweet and photo attached below. It is a piece of information learned through the expertise you are so willing to share. Finally, the message behind who you are and why you're here should be prominent throughout your portfolios on social media. Whether it be on Facebook, Twitter, or Instagram, visitors should easily be able to spot your message. In other words, the "who am I, why I'm here, and what I'm plugging."

Shannon's good friend Kyle Kittleson is an SEO (Search Engine Optimization) and social media expert, as well as a successful on-camera personality, host, and influencer. He has strong opinions on how to see those numbers go up rather than stay stagnant, or worse … decrease. Now you know why you want to be on social media, and it's time to establish a clear objective. As you start building your presence, it's time to take into consideration what you want from your followers. Do you want them to be a brand advocate for you? Is there a line of products for people to buy from you? Or is there a sign-up to your email list for an upcoming book, movie, or song to be on the lookout for? To optimize the success of their ultimate goal, many people will refer their followers to a personalized website that will further showcase an incentive to join a giveaway or opt into an email list. It's there that your audience can learn more about why you're here and what you bring to the table. Once you've filled all the nooks and crannies to your objective, you can now glance through the social media platforms and choose the one that best fits.

There are job postings all the time now for people to oversee a company's social media account. There's a reason for that. Simply put, making sure that all social media platforms are up-to-date and unique is a full-time job. So make sure to choose the platforms that you'll have time for, and please be picky. If you're a photographer, you wouldn't want your whole database to be on Twitter. Rather, Instagram and Pinterest would be the smarter choices. LinkedIn profiles are great for business consultants, and for those journalists out there, go ahead and tweet away throughout your day. Facebook, on the other hand, just happens to be its own special case where you can have both a personal page and a public Facebook page, otherwise known as a fan page. Now, if you believe being on all platforms is doable, you're in luck. Most platforms have the option to share your handles on your other social media profiles. Technology is so advanced that you can even link the post you shared to another platform. For example, if you share a photo on Instagram, that same photo can pop up on Twitter or Facebook. That's all good, sure. But in all honesty, having the same exact content is a bit of a bore. Give your viewers reasons to look at each platform through new and different content. Don't put all your eggs in one basket. Keep it simple, too, by making it easier for people to find you: using the same profile picture, header image, and username for each platform.

Though you "should" provide exclusive content on each page, it's important to stay consistent with your message and story. Stay true to who you are, they say! You can't be talking about politics on Twitter, while you're talking about the many ways to take care of your pet on Instagram, and then the many ways your boyfriend loves you on your Public Figure Facebook page. It'll just confuse viewers, who most of the time follow a particular page because it's showing or giving something they like or relate to. In essence, viewers won't know who you are and what they can count on you to deliver.

These social media pages are in all actuality like mini websites that require constant upkeep. Treat them as such. Some people don't completely fill out all the information a page suggests. Either that or they forget to update information that was once correct, but is no longer applicable (*are you really still in high school?*). After a quick glance through these simple "about-me" sections, a viewer will know right away if your page is worth scrolling over. "Pin your tweets" as the Twitterverse calls it, or "check the link in the bio" with Linktree as the Instagram users say. It's an easy and efficient way to gain traffic.

With that being said, the whole reason why you're back on social media is to really focus on adding value through whatever passion you have to offer the world. Creating anything without conscious intent will show as dispassionate, and viewers will be able to spot that right away. Those starting their journey in the social media world are incessantly pressing their audience to sign up for this product or read this article, which is perfectly okay every once in a while. It's a give-and-take relationship, a two-way street, but the giving must start first. The audience wants to see what you have to provide. Make sure to focus on bringing value in your field of choice. If you're a nutrition expert, post some smoothie recipes to make once a week. Tweet articles that have tips or professional advice for those viewers who came specifically to your page to lose weight—or whatever the case may be. Viewers love profiles that stay consistent with their content and brand.

One of the quickest ways to get more followers is to collaborate with social media influencers who have large followings. YouTubers are infamous for this very reason, as they all have a tight niche community solely because of these collaborations. For Instagram and Twitter users, the best way to make a collaboration is to first see what mutual friend you have with a user who has a big following. If you're in luck, utilize that connection and see if it's possible to "take over" that user's account. This works best if both parties have a similar brand. Let's assume your expertise is meditation and that the user you're collaborating with is a yoga guru. You can go ahead and roll out a series of Insta-stories about meditation in relation to his yoga session. Nowadays, many social media outlets even have the option to go "live." So, if taking over an account isn't possible, ask if the person can do a mini live session with you. Finding some way to collaborate can only prove beneficial, as it can expose you to a large audience while providing value for your new collaborator and expose him or her to a different audience.

We can take some of the tips we learned about actual on-camera training and apply them to how we navigate through social media, although there will no doubt be some modifications. Each world acts according to its own energy. There's a particular rhythm and current of influx and outflux. It is one that you'll have to learn how to dance and sing in, like all the other prominent figures in its space. In this case, that popular phrase "fake it 'til you make it" would not apply.

CHAPTER 15

THE WINNING FORMULA

The reasons, or the "why," cannot be emphasized enough when we're talking about the world of social media. The *why* you are here will be the *how* opportunities find you. Brands and companies tend to seek out those influencers whose message aligns most closely with theirs. Let us take a look at Instagram's top health and fitness influencer, Michelle Lewin. With a following base of about 13 million, you can bet that the companies looking for an alignment deal with her will be flushing out fitness caps and leggings that can stop the sweat from seeping through while you're squatting those 45lb plates. There might even be some makeup brands looking for her endorsement of a makeup that can last through that gruesome workout. But most of these companies will seek out Lewin particularly to reach that 13 million audience, who more than likely follow Lewin because they're interested in health and fitness. Maybe Lewin is too big of an example, as for some, she's practically considered a celebrity. But the trend still remains prevalent through the smaller scopes.

There have been nasty debates on whether social media is healthy, if it is here to stay, or even a good indication of real talent. However, there is no denying now that it is something to keep in mind. Before the technological era came around, celebrities rose to where they are now through their devastatingly good looks and charm, knowing the right people, having some degree of talent, and having a stroke of luck here and there. That is, if you believe in luck. But things took a turn—for the better or for the worse, you decide—and now the very same people who shot these celebrities to fame are seeking talent who also have a significant digital following. Earlier, we mentioned a few tips by Kyle Kittleson on how to jump-start your way into creating a firm foundation for your social media platform. But Kittleson also suspects that just like there is an algorithm to the way these outlets run their applications, there is also an algorithm we can take into consideration and study to optimize our results. There is what he called a formula.

He poses the question, "If you were looking for someone to rep your brand, would you take the person who is awesome on camera, or the person who is awesome on camera and has millions of loyal followers? I think we can all agree on the latter, even though there's a stubborn part of us that wants to clench onto the old way of doing things. But it is this same ability to reach and influence people from all over the world that is so valuable to companies and brands."

To Kittleson, there is a distinction that must be made between reach and influence, and how each of the two plays an important role in the social media dynamics. Reach is measured by how many people your messages come across to, while influence is how many people you can get to take action—whatever that may be. Think of it in terms of the two key factors we all learned in economics class: marketing and sales. You market to get the product known or out on the table and when it's time to start selling, you'll see just how successful your service is by how many people buy it. With the current climate, the balance must be scaled between reach and influence, because with balance comes a budding and gracious flow of supply and demand. The reach and influence categories both come with bolts that need to be screwed and tightened, because brands are quickly learning that a significant amount of reach (followers) does not correctly indicate any sort of positive return on their investment. If you can't get people to buy the product, then what's the point?

The point all circles back to the significant amount of influence a person has in his or her community. Companies are looking into what is called an engagement score to determine who can more successfully endorse a product. To obtain your engagement score, take a piece of content you have and its total number of engagements (E) and divide it by the total number of followers you have (F), which is expressed as a percentage known as your final score (S). The equation then stands as E/F=S. In this case scenario, we'll go ahead and use Instagram for our example since it seems to be the most popular choice of discussion. Say you post a photo (which is your piece of content) and it receives 200 likes, 100 comments, and 100 reposts. Your engagement total for that post will amount to 400 (200 + 100 + 100). At the particular time that you posted this image, you had 20,000 people following you. Go ahead and take that 400 and divide it by 20,000 to get your engagement score of 0.02, or 2 percent. Of course in reality, likes, comments, and shares don't have equal value to the algorithm. Comments have more weight than likes, etc. But this gives you a general idea.

Not too long ago, a score of 2 percent was perfectly acceptable. However, by Instagram standards, now an engagement percentage of over 3 percent is the minimum to be an influencer. And it looks like 10 to 15 percent is the norm of what's truly desirable by companies and brands. Note that I said "the norm," and not "good," because some companies might want a higher-than-normal engagement score. Whereas in all parts of society, "the norm" will undoubtedly change with time. Kittleson uses our pseudo-instafamous persons Mark and Andy to further demonstrate this ongoing reality.

"Suppose Mark has 100,000 Instagram followers and Andy has 20,000 Instagram followers. Based on this information, Mark would be a more attractive candidate. However, upon closer look we find that Mark's posts only get a few hundred likes, while Andy's get thousands of likes and comments ..." How could this be? Well, Andy has what Kittleson described as influence over his community or niche by engaging himself with his audience.

"He posts every day and takes advantage of all the mediums Instagram has within itself. While on the other hand, it's been months since Mark has posted anything. Even though Mark has five times as much reach as Andy, Andy has a much larger influence, or ability to persuade his audience to action. He will therefore be the most viable candidate for a product endorsement deal due to the amount of engagement he has with his followers."

When someone comments on your Instagram, do you respond? No? Well, you should. And ideally within twenty-four hours. When someone follows you on Twitter, do you introduce yourself? No? Well, think about it. When someone shares your Facebook post, do you give that person a shout-out? No? Well, seems like the polite thing to do, right? And this all doesn't cancel out the fact that you need to get as many followers as you can. You really do, but hike up that engagement score and you'll be on your way to sign a deal with that company you've been meaning to do business with.

With all things, there are always some levels of cons to weigh. I say this not to further discourage you, but to further expand your knowledge of the world you're about to dive into. According to *Forbes* magazine, there are some downsides to take into consideration. In most cases, it's hard to get an accurate account of return on investment, as most of it is very much self-reported. So, make sure that the research going into your investment is thorough and clean. One of the last few mentionings by *Forbes* is that some industries are better suited for social media marketing than others. Any company that specifically ties high-resolution photos or imaging into their brand can see a better ROI than other companies. This particular growth that everyone wants in the media world requires, in essence, some good luck.

Amy Johnson, Founder of Personal Producers and Executive Director of Master & Muse by supermodel and actress Amber Valletta, shares a personal experience about a time when the use of social media was, in the simplest terms, unavoidable. Amber decided to jump into the pool of entrepreneurship to start a business in sustainable fashion—combining her love of fashion with her love of the environment. At the time, social media was on the rise, but it was not clear how advantageous social media would be in this endeavor. After a memorable meeting at the CAA Foundation, Amy and Amber decided that they were going to promote Master & Muse through social media.

Amber, who now has close to 425,000 (and growing) Instagram followers, literally burst into tears during the meeting, at the thought of having to start engaging on social media. This was an understandable reaction, considering how vast, vague, and challenging it was to navigate those unchartered waters at that time. Amber, however, was committed to her business and the important cause. Amber and Amy surrendered to the flow, took the route that was suggested and forged ahead to prove to themselves, and others, that one didn't have to sacrifice style for substance. But what was it that ultimately caused the two business owners to keep going?

The answer is simple: passion and purpose. Amy and Amber believe strongly in utilizing business to do good in the world. Fashion is known as one of the dirtiest industries in the world, with its long supply chains, tendency towards overproduction, immense waste, toxic practices and cheap labor—the fashion industry contributes much to the growing global climate crisis. With that said, fashion is also a creative and aspirational industry that loves a challenge. It was evident to both Amy and Amber that starting a company out of core values and positive intentions would create a domino effect and inevitably begin to shift this resource intensive industry in a new, sustainable direction.

There is a rise in corporations and brands that are starting to take into consideration what Amy said is called the Triple Bottom Line (profit / planet / people). In other words, businesses that look at the monetary gains and costs of providing a product or service, as well as evaluating the bottom line impact their business has on people and the planet. Amy and Amber take the Triple Bottom Line thinking into account when making decisions on how to conduct business, something that they believe is necessary in any line of work. Using the lens of the Master & Muse core values, Amy developed a vetting system for making decisions "it may save money to take an action, but if we are causing harm to the planet or people, we won't do it. It may take longer to accomplish our goals, but it's worth it. We are in it for the long haul." She followed up with a favorite quote from Ghandi: "There is no beauty in the finest cloth if it brings hunger and unhappiness."

According to Amy, "There is a changing dynamic to our world's celebrities and influencers. The particular power they hold is changing at lightning speed. Though we still look to celebrities to lead us when we feel lost, confused or desperate in difficult times, the younger generations unabashedly seek authenticity. They are able to discern who is real and who isn't."

In describing Amber's authentic appeal, Amy coined the phrase the "valued influencer" to describe a celebrity or influencer whose lifestyle and values match what she puts out in the world and communicates on all her channels.

"These types of celebrities are a force," Amy states, "they boldly speak from their values and provide a voice for those afraid or who aren't able to speak up—that includes the earth! Keen on spotting inauthenticity, the younger generations are looking for society's 'creative connectors' who are in alignment with their values, to lead the way!

"Amber and I have been committed to spreading the message #buybetter in the most effective way possible. We are encouraging an educated buyer to make informed and better decisions when purchasing. We've all learned to do this with our food, now we want to help shoppers do this with their clothes." Amy continues, "The valued influencer, like Amber, plays a key role in educating and engaging the consumer, which helps people feel empowered when buying."

Instagram provides a great communication outlet for this messaging. Whereas on television everything must be polished and perfect, Instagram allows for more freedom of expression and raw reality—while still looking good.

While it's common practice that businesses seek out numbers to determine who should be the new voice of their brand, Amy reckons that this is beginning to change, as brands are also going to have consider different factors to ensure brand loyalty.

"The values of the influencers they choose to work with will need to align with their own values and products. The influencers themselves have a lot more influence on the brands than they even realize. Many have the power to ask a brand to be more sustainable. These influencers can lead the brands to do the right thing and in so doing, build loyal customers that care," says Amy

A formula that Amy said will prove more efficient to engage the consumer in a purposeful way: Responsible Brand + Valued Influencer (lives what he/she posts) + Product Story (how a product is made) = Consumer that is engaged, educated, and loyal. To survive in the increasingly competitive world, brands will have to consider more than an influencers numbers on Instagram, they will have to pay attention to the integrity of their products, services and values of their influencers. Customer loyalty and brand value will drive the success of their business, because no business wants to end up like that corner shop on the street that seems to be constantly changing from a home furniture store to a fusion restaurant. It's time to stick around.

A main component to being on-camera ready for Guestperts, and for those just seeking some media training, is to make sure the information you provide through whatever outlet is accurate. Whether it be an actual television appearance or a live story shot on Instagram, portraying yourself in the right light is essential to stable success. These small factors of presenting yourself in the right light with consistency, credibility and accuracy all add up to the crucial question at hand: *are you likable?*

Samantha Boardman, M.D., wrote an article in *Psychology Today* called "Do You Have #hashtag Friends or Real Friends?" The article marks a significant link between popularity and our very own well-being through a compilation of research and interviews from people within the field of psychology. In our world today, it is hard to differentiate between the two kinds of popularity that seem to keep us going when the going gets rough. After all, the heavy weight on our shoulders seems less of a burden when there's someone to share it with.

Likability and status are two very different planes in which people operate. Boardman cites Professor of Psychology and Neurology Mitch Prinstein to further differentiate the effects of what it means to be likable versus have status. The "distinction between likability and status is an important one. Likes on Facebook have nothing to do with likability. Likability is predicated on making an effort, on being responsive, and understanding. A likable person is an 'active catalyst' of goodness. The wise words of John Templeton come to mind: 'It's nice to be important, but it's more important to be nice.' "

In other words, the topic of genuineness cannot be denied and needs further emphasis in this digital day and age. To be likable means to function from the inner being of your truest self—that divinity in you and everyone else. Aiming to be a person of significant status will inevitably lead you down a never-ending path. People with this goal strive for influence and power—validated through their number of followers. Likable people operate their behaviors under everything that falls under the category of genuine love and passion for what they do. To be this type of person can lead not only to advantages in your career prospects, but to friendships that last through those sick days where loneliness seems to be the only friend you have.

Viewers, as we discussed, can easily sniff out influencers who genuinely care or don't care about what they're putting out for the public to see. It is noticeable in both the content itself and everything that surrounds it. Every single media outlet can help obtain followers and cultivate a social media presence. But I'm sure you've heard of that quintessential karmic lesson: you get what you give. It is a balance of energy. For example, famous YouTubers take extra care and precaution in making sure that their video series are edited to perfection—even to the very last second. A video filmed on an iPhone in your apartment with little to no editing and the sun obnoxiously leaching out the color of your skin does not equate to a successful segment of the demo reel you planned on submitting to that television network.

Susan Gold, executive of SusanGoldConsulting.com, actually closed a deal with celebrity influencer and artist Andy Warhol. She was living a few blocks away from Andy's studio at the time when Donny Deutsch wanted Warhol to endorse one of his clients, a tri-state New York Pontiac Dealership, in a commercial. Deutsch was running his dad's advertising agency in Manhattan, and Gold built up the courage to walk down and see what she could make happen. Andy's manager, Fred, answered the door, and she nervously asked if she could schedule a meeting with Andy about the possibility of doing a television commercial. To make a long story short, Gold walked into Andy's studio the very next day and Andy's hair itself was a work of art, going in all sorts of directions. The frantic artist didn't even look up to make eye contact with the nervous Gold, but there was an opportunity in the moment when Gold noticed that Andy was surrounded by pugs, and she pitched him the idea that his very own dogs could be in the Pontiac commercials. That particular deal put Gold on the map professionally. She described how ad agencies play a crucial role in helping an influencer come to life. They can build their client up and make the influencer even bigger and more legitimate for all businesses involved.

Perhaps that fine balance of old and new will never go away. But Gold did leave us with gracious advice for up-and-coming experts looking to jump into the influencer arena. She notes that "influencers can be just on social media, but experts need to have blogs, socials, books, media presence, etc. These days TV and social media are all colliding. I will say that an expert does need a website if they want to do TV and influencers really don't need that ... more and more people are going to try to be influencers for capital reasons. And more people will see how much work it takes ..."

Alara Ceri, a social media influencer turned social media manager in Los Angeles, California, handles more than twenty clients that are influencers and micro-influencers. Her own personal experiences have led her clients to great success that include alignment deals, product endorsements, and call-ins from networks, studios, and production companies for show consideration. She says that in social media, there are no shortcuts. Content, content, content is the biggest success contributor in the social media world, but it is not so much *what* you post—though, in some cases, it is—as *how* you post your content. Ceri advises her clients to put out content at least five times a week, and to only post content they are passionate about and that brings value to their audience.

"You are the CEO of your social platform. It is now your brand and company. People are going to your page to get something from you. If you treat your company with that level of responsibility, then putting out valuable content on a daily basis will become second nature for you," states Ceri.

Shift that mind set from hobby to business. And in a business, technicalities are just as important to the final product.

Ceri describes one trick that will determine whether your page becomes a hit or a miss: "The easier you make it for someone to understand your page at first sight, the faster they'll follow you."

This is what she calls "the theme," and for those of you looking to establish yourselves in social media, stick to about three or four themes for your page. It's quite different from a message or niche, as a theme is rather what your page comprises as a whole—what a viewer can see just by looking at your page. As a social influencer for "Artists of Hollywood," Ceri's themes include sketch comedy videos of her art, snapshots of her and her personal adventures, and quotes or memes that relate to being an artist.

"I entertain people with my art, I open up to people by sharing my personal life, and I give my opinions through quotes or memes that relate to being a female artist in Hollywood," says Alara.

She makes her page personal, as that is one of her themes, yet there are few photos of her family, friends, or husband, which are included only if they somehow tie into her theme or brand at hand. And as mentioned, watching the masters at work is one of the greatest educations, so go ahead and take a look at some of your own favorite influencers and see if you can pick out their themes and why one page seems more successful than another.

Aesthetics also come into play when creating a successful social media platform. Color palette is very much a characteristic to take into consideration. In general, we naturally turn toward colors that look more attractive and appealing to the eye. As a female artist in Hollywood, Ceri's preferred color that pops in her mind is hot pink. She uses this to her advantage; with each quote she posts, she uses a pink background. And with each video or picture, it's brightened to match that color texture of pink. Convey your personality on your page for your followers to see. Pink and bright is exactly how Ceri envisions Hollywood and her personality to be.

Since you are the CEO of your page, you are also the creative director and have full creative control over all the fine details that go into that page. If you want your page to have a more minimalistic style, make sure that you tie it into your theme, brand, and message. Make these traits align. And those favorite influencers I told you to take a look at? They more likely than not have their own clear color scheme.

"The more specific you are with every part of your social media, the more you'll grow it and become a respected brand other influencers would want to work with. We can't look at a red bull's-eye sign without thinking 'Target' ... make that same distinction for your page," says Ceri.

For those of you who are complete control freaks like me, delving into your statistics and analytics can be great if you know how to interpret them. Posting five times a week like Ceri suggested will not only engage your audience with who you are and what you're doing, but it is also a way to see what posts are getting the most traction and when. Each social media platform uses a different algorithm. For example, for many Instagram users, posting on Saturday around 2 p.m. might be great, whereas posting constantly only Monday through Friday on Twitter might be better for those who use that platform. Yet, within these different algorithms, there is still a bit of a complication. A lot of that engagement is trackable, so you can find trends to use to your advantage. Conduct your research into your highest-engaging posts through likes, comments, or subscriptions, because within each brand or niche, the ideal time of day to post will vary. "It's five o'clock somewhere," as Ceri so cleverly puts it.

While social media algorithms can help direct your page to another person whose interests seem to align with yours, if you're worried that someone overseas won't see your page, make sure to utilize some hashtags that tie into your niche. Stay relevant and stay on top of it, because we're #InItToWinIt.

Here is a list of apps that Ceri suggests using if you want to fine-tune your pages for your journey toward becoming an Instagram influencer:

Social Upgrade, Social Steeze, Social Drift, Ampfluence, Social Buddy, Social Growth, Campfire, Social Envy: These are all social media growth services.

Wordswag: Creates posters, beautiful posts for announcements, giveaways, etc.

Facetune: Great for photoshopping. Ideal for aspiring fashion and beauty influencers.

"LIKE" App: Provides special effects for videos. Think green screen and backgrounds.

Crowdfire (Twitter) and Cleaner (Instagram): Known as "unfollow" apps, to clean house on pages that you are following that no longer follow you.

Whitegram: Fits your pictures to the Instagram screen.

Lightroom and VSCO: Give photos a distinct touch with fantastic lighting and color options.

iMovie App: For iPhone users, this app is the easiest way to edit your videos for Instagram. You can film and edit right from your phone.

Alara Ceri sees that the influencer space will only continue to grow from here. "It is a place that many people, companies, and brands are continuing to realize just how beneficial it can be to their advertising strategies. What could be better than free advertising? It started from our personal AIM chat rooms to Tom's clever Myspace to the largest platform in existence, Facebook ... and beyond!

"It's an intimate place to share not only our own personal hero's journey but also an ultimate place of marginalized consumerism. We went from 'who does she think she is?' to 'wow, she made herself famous off Instagram' because anyone with a good idea and a clever and/or stylish execution can build themselves an income off of their social media. It is now an occupation for many, and for some their only source of income that can sustain all their living expenses and even buy that fancy Mercedes they've always been wanting."

Ceri leaves us with a warning, if we hope to make a dent in the social media market: "Though you are free to create anything you want as this is your creative space, the more people who become famous here the more people want to do it. Competition increases and stakes grow higher. Anything less than an A-game influencer will be quietly forgotten in the depths as if your page never even existed. If you treat your social media—and everything in life—as an Olympian athlete of the internet, you'll strike gold."

It goes to show us that anything in this realm can't be done halfway nowadays. No more beating around the bush, because hard work and dedication will surely be the winner.

Give yourself a pat on the back because you're not only an expert in your topic of choice, but you're now an expert and commander-in-chief of your own social media portfolio. And if you are hosting your content, well then, you are a host as well. Here comes the best part: since you're established as one of these so-called social media influencers, it's time to set your price rate. A common number I hear is that you should charge $20 to $40 per thousand followers if a brand wants you to do a project for them. Remember, you're not a celebrity yet, so negotiations can be weighed to a certain degree. Work out a deal with a long-term proposal versus a one-time post and what it entails. It could potentially include videos, still photos, live-streaming with links, hashtags, or general brand mentions. The whole shebang! As these posts go lower into your feed, the more power they lose. But the bright side is that they're still there to be found, so go ahead and try working out a timeline for how long a post should be up and maybe a discounted weekly rate to keep that post up for a given period of time. Twenty to forty percent of your initial charge per week is suggested, all according to the number of followers you have.

This is truly a time like no other. It's amazing how people can create a name for themselves and have the autonomy to really get themselves on a never-ending map. However, you could argue that the downside is pretty substantial, as well. We are so overwhelmed with content that no one knows what to really focus on. We are constantly bombarded with images, colors, and information so vast that it's probably pretty unhealthy and unsustainable. I mean, can our brains really hold all of that, let alone process it? Not only are our brains being overloaded, but our industry is slowly toppling under the weight of the social media giants. Networks, studios, production companies, etc. are so freaked out by this new wave and are scrambling to find ways to be like Kelly Slater and ride it! And one of the major ways we are seeing them do this is by hiring really young, often unqualified people that they hope will have their finger on the pulse of this ever-changing world.

Unfortunately, there is something humbling about working your way to the top that is being lost with this wave of youth in high-end and high-paying jobs who just don't understand because they haven't lived it. Climb the ladder and you'll eventually get to the top. I know this makes me sound old, and maybe being in your late thirties is old, but seeing people in their mid-to-late twenties as heads of development is in a sense quite troubling. Yes, call me grandma, but I miss the way it used to be—dealing with people who have years of experience under their belt in positions of authority and importance.

Be prepared if you make it to the place in your career as an influencer where you have HUGE representation at a major agency that your agent might be your age ... Or younger! It's interesting times for sure.

LEXICON

Agent: A person who finds jobs for talent and receives a percentage commission from the salary earned by the talent for the on-air job that was found by them.

Audition: A performance interview for talent to see if they are the right fit for the on-camera job.

Banter: On-camera extemporaneous talk between talent that is not written in the script, usually used as a tool to fill air time.

Being green: An industry terminology used to describe new or naive talent that doesn't have experience on air or on set.

Board: Written script, with a sharpie typically on easel paper found in presentations attached to a stand that is near eye level of the camera, for actors or hosts to use when they need help with lines during an audition. Similar to a Cue card.

Branding: A business term to describe the creation of an image or perception to the public of an influencer, a company, a product or a service.

Brand message: The content message behind an image or a perception to the public in order to communicate an idea, concept or call to action.

Break: Short form for commercial break between segments of a program whether television, radio, or podcast.

B-roll: A layer of B footage in film or on television that gives a dimensional video impression without sound to the A story being conveyed.

Call sheet: A list of producers names, talent names, drive on permissions, contact information and schedule for the entire production crew on set for a daily shoot.

Camera ready: This means that talent has been made up by professional hair and makeup artists for the purposes of being taped, filmed, or photographed.

Content: The information accumulated and written down by a producer for a script.

Copy/Sides: Another word for the script that a talent will perform on camera.

Creative connector: An influencer that connects people to products or services in a fun creative and unique way that is specific to their own branding.

Cue: A visual or audio indication to notify the talent to start their content while cameras are recording.

Cue card: Stock board with handwritten scripting for talent held by a stage manager or producer next to the recording camera.

Director: A television director executes the on-air production based on scripts and rundowns provided by the show's producer.

Editorial: A statement of opinion by a particular form of media i.e., print, radio, or television. It can be a statement of opinion by the actual medium itself i.e., The *LA Times.*

Eye-line: Where the talent looks in relationship to the camera lens. The camera crew knows not to walk or distract the talent from their eye-line which is their focus to camera.

Fix it in post: When something is not totally perfect during a shoot, it is corrected in post-production (editing). This can happen in a live to tape, but not in a live taping.

Focus: Having the main person or element of a shot be clear and sharp so the viewer knows what to pay attention to during the segment.

Green room: The backstage space for guests to gather, wait, dress, and mentally prepare before a show or appearance. This is where the talent will meet the producer, sign a release form, and get mic'd by the sound technician.

Hard out: A firm and fixed time ending in a program.

Headshots: Professional pictures for acquiring work for hosts or booking opportunities for guests.

Hit time: The time you are actually on air during a segment.

Homebase: On stage of a television studio show in contrast to sitting in the audience of the television studio show.

Host: A guide, emcee, moderator, or interviewer for an on-camera, podcast, television or radio program.

IFB: Stands for either "Interrupt for Broadcast" or "Interruptible Feedback/Foldback." This is the inner-ear device that many hosts use to hear direction from producers while on air.

Influencers: Individuals who have the power to affect purchase decisions of others because of their (real or perceived) authority, knowledge, position, or relationship in the social media space.

Intro: A script reference for what a host reads to open a segment on air.

Jargon: Synonymous with vernacular. See Vernacular.

Kit: Short for lighting kit or makeup kit. It's what production professionals refer to as their gear of trade.

Languaging: Creating simple explanations for complicated concepts in speaking points.

Lavalier (lav) v. handheld mic: The two main types of microphones a host will use on camera. A lavalier microphone will be attached to your wardrobe as close to your mouth as possible, and a handheld mic will be held in your hand. The host is responsible for proper mic technique. Understanding the differences is significant for both a host and a guest so the camera can capture good sound when a person is talking or being interviewed.

Man-on-the-street: An interview style that happens on location in a public place for hosts to interview passersby with pop-culture and/or largely humorous questions for the purpose of entertaining viewing audiences.

Mark: The piece of tape on a floor that a talent or a host stands on that was pre-set, usually by the director, for the purposes of being set to camera framing and focus, usually in the shape of a T or X.

Memorization: The process of committing content, scripts, or lines to memory.

Nuance: A slight difference in appearance, meaning, tape, or sound that throws the perfection of the production off, even by a frame or an audio blip.

On-air: Being broadcast live on radio or television.

Opening sound bite: Your first statement during an appearance that includes who you are; what you will be telling us about; why you are a legitimate voice in your space; and what we can count on you to deliver.

Outlet: The broadcast center associated with a television show, network, or studio.

Outro: A script cue that a host uses for the close of a segment.

PA: Short for production assistant. This is a member of a film or TV crew who is responsible for assisting in various tasks of a production. The PA reports to a producer of various titles.

Package: An insert of a full story within a show or segment, even if this full story is only thirty seconds long. It's a visual and audio storytelling compilation meant to support the overall show or segment in which it is placed.

Performance: The act of executing or delivering an appearance on a show or program, whether live or live-to-tape.

Producer: In this book, we affectionately refer to the producer as the composer of a segment or a show. The producer pulls in all elements, talent, and aspects that make a show or a segment happen.

Publicist: A professional who serves to book clients on a variety of media outlets.

Questions: The content the host will ask that is usually derived from the speaking points provided by the guest in an interview format.

Rehearsal: A practice performance or on-camera training.

ROI: Return on Investment. The performance measurement used to determine the value, feedback, and the worth of money spent for a specific outcome.

Segment: A short-form slot of programming within a show.

Set: The stage or location where filming or taping takes place.

Speaking points: The content a guest is expected to deliver on air, based on an unspoken agreement between that guest, the producer, and the show.

Social media: A variety of platforms through websites or applications that allow collective networking to occur over the internet.

Sound bite: A short extract from a recorded interview, chosen for its wit.

Sound check: A rehearsal of sound technology and equipment for perfection before an actual performance.

Stand-up: A host delivers information directly to the camera while standing up. This is often a reporter's technique for being in the field.

Take: A singular filmed version of a particular shot or setup.

Talking points: See Speaking Points.

Teleprompter: The technology used for a host to read a script directly to the camera.

Throw: The verbal technique a host uses to shift to a co-host, using phrases like, "Let's go to John in the field to get a report on the weather …"

Toss: The verbal technique a host uses to exit a television segment or move to another part of the show. The host tosses to either a package, a B-roll, an interview, or a commercial break. Phrases like "Coming up next," "When we return," and "We need to take a break" are all examples of tosses.

Underperforming: The failure of talent to put their full potential into their appearance because of having low energy, being underprepared, or playing it safe.

Unscripted TV: Unscripted television falls into the categories of news, talk shows, reality shows, and magazine shows. Although it is considered unscripted, all producers at the very least use rough lines and story arcs to script.

Valued influencer: An influencer (celebrity or not) who has sway of public opinion through their strong and specific point of view.

Vernacular: Industry terminology like this list of words we are outlining right here.

Wardrobe: The clothing worn on camera.

Wrap: The end of a shoot, a shot, or a show.

Xenagogy: A guidebook. Like the one you are reading right now!

Yes... and: For a guest expert this is an expression of pivot to be used while speaking on air to redirect the flow of conversation back to your speaking points. "Yes" I've heard you and "And" this is what I am going to contribute from my speaking points. Hosts also use "Yes... and" during interviews to incorporate the answers they receive into their next question and while co-hosting to make the dynamic with their fellow host more conversational.

Zebra: A lighting terminology.

Zoom: To focus a camera iris tighter.

ABOUT THE AUTHOR

JACQUIE JORDAN

Jacquie Jordan is the founder of the fifteen-year-old Silicon Beach–based TVGuestpert, TVGuestpert Publishing and TVOnCameraTraining.com. TVGuestpert is a media development company that raises the profile of the Guestpert in the media and grows their client's core business. With TVGuestpert, Jacquie works with businesses on their branding, promotion, marketing, producing and development, as well as their on-camera execution.

Jacquie has been involved in booking, supervising or producing as many as 10,000+ television guests. Her reign has come from successfully launching and executing many syndicated daytime programs and cable shows. Known for her ability to find the heart of any story, Jacquie garnered her second Daytime Emmy nomination for Best Show on *Donny & Marie* (Sony Pictures Television).

Jacquie's foray in talent comes from her time in the trenches as a nationally recognized producer in broadcast television. As Showrunner of the long running AMC series *Sunday Morning Shootout*, hosted by Hollywood icons, Chair of Mandalay Entertainment, Peter Guber and Former Editor-in-Chief of Variety, Peter Bart. Celebrity guests produced by Jacquie include Steven Spielberg, Charlize Theron, Clint Eastwood, Angelina Jolie, Peter Jackson, George Clooney and Dustin Hoffman.

Simultaneously, as Executive Producer, Jacquie launched the copycat formula of *Shootout* for the TVGuide Channel, *Square-Off* with a focus on the television industry hosted by Andy Wallenstein and Brian Lowry of Variety. Jacquie vetted the best the industry had to offer—from NBC head Ben Silverman, Shonda Rhimes to known television stars like Jon Cryer and Mark Harmon.

As a *New York Times* bestselling publisher, *Publisher's Weekly* is quoted as saying, "Jordan seems to have succeeded at her goal as laid out on the TVGuestpert website," when talking about the success of The TVGuestpert Publishing orchestrated, *The Art of Having It All* hitting the coveted list.

As the author of *Get on TV! The Insider's Guide to Pitching the Producers and Promoting Yourself!* (Sourcebooks 2006) and *Heartfelt Marketing: Allowing the Universe to Be Your Business Partner* (BurmanBooks 2010), she has been featured in *Entrepreneur* magazine, *Selling Power* magazine, *Feedback* magazine, *Emmy* magazine, and the cover of *Woman's World* magazine. As a commentator on television regarding the business of the industry and pop culture, Jacquie's appearances include Fox Reality, Good Day New York, Fox, ABC Family, CBS's Big Shot Live, TV Guide Channel, CBS Evening News, FX and countless radio shows. Jacquie is a graduate of the University of Delaware, with a B.A. in Communications and a minor in theater.

She currently resides in Los Angeles spending her free time practicing yoga, raising awareness around animal neglect and mentoring women entrepreneurs.

JJordan@TVGuestpert.com

TVGuestpert.com

@TVGuestpert

ABOUT THE AUTHOR

SHANNON O'DOWD

Shannon O'Dowd is a TV Host/Spokesperson as well as an on-camera coach and media trainer who specializes in TV hosts, influencers, and experts. Originally from St. Petersburg, FL with a degree in Theatre Performance from Florida State University, she has been working on both sides of the camera (as on-camera host and also as a coach), for well over a decade.

As on-camera talent, she has been the spokesperson for several national commercial campaigns including Cable One, Sunsweet Raisins, OfficeMax, Invisalign, and Nissan. As a host, she has been on QVC as well as being the face of many spots in the infomercial world including Keurig, Aerobed, Instant Figure, Nano Gym, Lipozene, and Bankruptcy Legal Network.

As a coach, she has clients on the Today Show, the Doctors, HGTV, Hallmark, WE, DIY, QVC, HSN, and on talk shows, news appearances, morning shows, and more! Her training focuses on-camera technique, brand messaging, talking points, and sound bites for TV Appearances, Press Junkets, Talk Shows, Social Media, etc. Shannon specializes in getting the best performance possible out of her clients with spot-on adjustments and information that "sticks" and aids in many areas, even beyond just on-camera work. Shannon is precise, insightful, fun, and great at getting the best performance possible from her clients.

hello@Shannonodowd.com

ShannonODowd.com

@theshannonodowd

TVGUESTPERT PUBLISHING

JACK H. HARRIS
Father of the Blob: The Making of a Monster Smash and Other Hollywood Tales
Paperback: $16.95
Kindle/Nook: $9.99

New York Times Best Seller
CHRISTY WHITMAN
The Art of Having It All: A Woman's Guide to Unlimited Abundance
Paperback: $16.95
Kindle/Nook: $9.99
Audible Book: $13.00

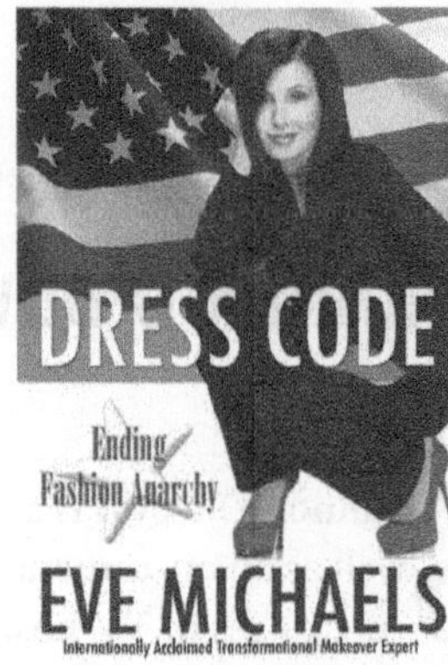

EVE MICHAELS
Dress Code: Ending Fashion Anarchy
Paperback: $15.95
Kindle/Nook: $9.99
Audible Book: $17.95

DARREN CAMPO
Alex Detail's Revolution
Paperback: $9.95
Hardcover: $22.95
Kindle: $9.15

DARREN CAMPO
Alex Detail's Rebellion
Hardcover: $22.95
Kindle: $9.99

DARREN CAMPO
Disappearing Spell: Generationist Files: Book 1
Kindle: $2.99

TVGuestpert Publishing
11664 National Blvd, #345
Los Angeles, CA. 90064
310-584-1504
www.TVGPublishing.com

GAYANI DeSILVA, MD
A Psychiatrist's Guide: Stop Teen Addiction Before It Starts
Paperback: $16.95
Kindle: $9.99

GAYANI DeSILVA, MD
A Psychiatrist's Guide: Helping Parents Reach Their Depressed Tween
Paperback: $16.95
Kindle: $9.99

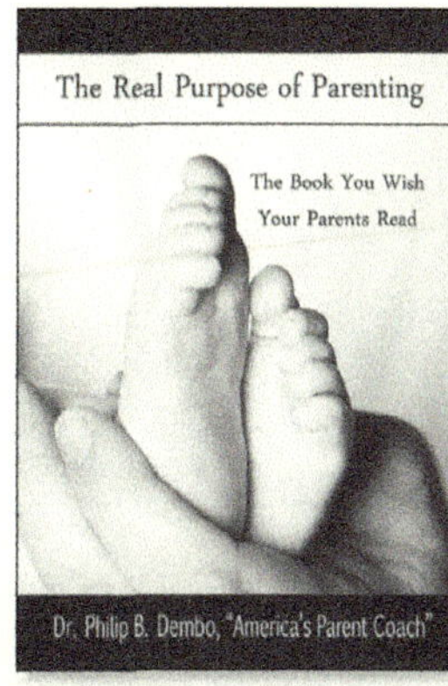

DR. PHILIP DEMBO
The Real Purpose of Parenting: The Book You Wish Your Parents Read
Paperback: $15.95
Kindle: $9.99
Audible: $23.95

JACQUIE JORDAN AND SHANNON O'DOWD
*The Ultimate On-Camera Guidebook: Hosts*Experts*Influencers*
Paperback: $16.95
Kindle: $9.99

JACQUIE JORDAN
Heartfelt Marketing: Allowing the Universe to be Your Business Partner
Paperback: $15.95
Kindle: $9.99
Audible: $9.95

JACQUIE JORDAN
Get on TV! The Insider's Guide to Pitching the Producers and Promoting Yourself
Published by Sourcebooks
Paperback: $14.95
Kindle: $9.99
Nook: $14.95